The Tragical History
of
Doctor Faustus

Crofts Classics

GENERAL EDITOR

Samuel H. Beer, *Harvard University*

CHRISTOPHER MARLOWE

The
Tragical History
of Doctor Faustus

EDITED BY

Paul H. Kocher

STANFORD UNIVERSITY

Harlan Davidson, Inc.
Wheeling, Illinois 60090-6000

Library of Congress Cataloging-in-Publication Data

Marlowe, Christopher, 1564–1593.
   Doctor Faustus: the tragical history of Doctor Faustus /
   Christopher Marlowe ; edited by Paul H. Kocher.
   p. cm. — (Crofts classics)
   Bibliography: p 63.
   ISBN 0-88295-054-1
   1. Faust, d. ca. 1540—Drama. I. Kocher, Paul Harold, 1907–.
II. Title.
PR2664.A2K64   1989
882'.3–dc20   89–34291
                                                     CIP

Manufactured in the United States of America
01 00 99 98 97 49 CM

INTRODUCTION

Date, Authorship, and Text. Like many other dates
concerning Marlowe's work, the year in which *Doctor Faustus* was written and first performed is un-
certain. Conjecture has ranged between 1588 and
1592, but the weight of evidence seems to favor the
former date. *Faustus* was, then, probably the second
of Marlowe's great plays, coming in 1588 immediately after *Tamburlaine*. The fact that the English
translation of the German Faust story, the source
from which Marlowe drew most of the material for
his play, has survived only in an edition published
in 1592 might appear to require a later dating. But
the statement on the title page of this 1592 edition
that it was "Newly imprinted, and in convenient
places imperfect matter amended" suggests an earlier edition, to which, indeed, there are references
in contemporary works by Gabriel Harvey, Henry
Holland, and others before 1590. Likewise a ballad
published in February, 1589, on "the life and death
of Doctor Faustus, the great Conjuror" seems to have
been based on Marlowe's drama. And the style of the
play, together with its frequent allusions to university life and learning, marks it as belonging probably
to a period soon after Marlowe's graduation from
Cambridge in 1587.

Presumably *Faustus* was first performed in 1588
when it was written. We know also from the diary of
the Elizabethan manager and promoter, Philip Henslowe, that it was revived in the autumn of 1594 by

the Lord Admiral's Men with the brilliant tragedian Edward Alleyn in the title role. It was acted again several times during the next few years but not published until 1604, when the first edition was printed by Valentine Simmes. Reprints of this edition came out in 1609 and 1611. Then in 1616 appeared an edition differing in many important respects from that of 1604. It contained many new scenes and many changes in the old ones. The modern editor is obliged to decide which of these two versions represents most closely the play as Marlowe wrote it. The present edition is based primarily on the 1604 text, although in a few individual passages the 1616 reading has been adopted. Not that the 1604 text is anything like perfect. It seems in truth to have been printed from a manuscript which had been badly garbled by actors and revisers during the many performances staged since 1588. But it takes us as close as we can get today to the form Marlowe intended.

That Marlowe ever wrote any of the comic prose scenes in *Faustus* looks extremely doubtful. The blank verse scenes are certainly from his pen, as also is the serious prose of Scene Fourteen, but the comic prose seems to have been written by some other dramatist, perhaps by Thomas Nashe, Marlowe's friend, who also collaborated with Marlowe on the earlier tragedy of *Dido*. Marlowe was perfectly capable of humor, but his vein had a rather heavy, sardonic, intellectual quality not to be found in the comic prose of the play. On the other hand, Nashe's prose pamphlets contain many specific resemblances in content and in nimbleness of style to the scenes of the Pope, the Horse-courser, the Seven Deadly Sins and the rest. If someone other than Marlowe wrote these scenes, the next question is whether they were a part of the original play or were added at some later date. Perhaps it is most likely that they were not put into the play until it was revived for performance after the plague in 1594. Mention in Scene XI of Doctor Lopez, who was executed in 1594, is strong evidence in this direction. The question, however, can not yet be definitely answered. We know also that in 1602 Henslowe paid the dramatists William Birde and Samuel Rowley £4 "for their additions in Doctor Faustus." But these additions seem not to have been printed in the 1604 text of the play. They appeared instead in the 1616 text, and consisted of new serious blank verse and comic prose scenes of inferior quality. These have been omitted from the present edition.

Sources and Interpretation. In Marlowe's day it was the custom for playwrights to get their plots from old stories or plays previously written. Marlowe founded his drama mainly on the legend of a German magician as told in the *Historia von D. Johann Fausten,* first published at Frankfurt in 1587 and soon afterwards translated into English prose by one "P. F., Gent." as *The Historie of the damnable life and deserved death of Doctor John Faustus.* Marlowe knew only this English translation, not the German original. There had actually lived a scholar named Faust in Germany early in the sixteenth century who, by the usual working of popular superstition, had acquired a reputation for magic because of his learning. Around his name had collected scores of exploits commonly attributed to magicians not only during the Renaissance but during the Middle Ages and back to the classical period. The story of his life was moralized into a struggle between the forces of good and evil in which Faustus, failing to repent of his black art practiced through the Devil, must finally lose his soul.

Marlowe came across the English translation soon after it was published. He saw in it the possibilities for high dramatic tension, his imagination leaped to the wonder and terror of the deeds of magic, and the religious conflict drew powerfully on feelings which he was undergoing in his own life. It was for him the perfect theme. He set to work on it with a grasp of intellect and a controlled splendor of poetry which he showed in no other play. The English translation —call it the English Faust Book—presented him with a large number of short chapters detailing the events of Faustus' temptation, fall, and traffic with the demons, a narrative not altogether wanting in power but long-winded, disorganized, and without any supreme touch of imagination or insight into character. Marlowe made no alterations in the larger outlines of the plot. But his changes in depth of conception and in the handling of details afford the best of lessons in the art of dramaturgy. Thus he omitted altogether many incidents like those relating Faustus' journeys to hell, to the garden of Eden, to numerous foreign lands; other incidents he compressed; a few he expanded. His choice in every such case was determined by the degree of dramatic point in the incident and its adaptability to the resources of the Elizabethan stage. Succinct dialogue, lacking in the source, he supplied with that fine terseness which always marked his best work. On the debit side, however, too faithful a following of the thread of events in the source seems to have betrayed Marlowe into the major weakness of his play. As in the English Faust Book, so in the play, there is a falling off in dramatic interest between the time of Faustus' signing of the contract and the expiration of its twenty-four years. Faustus wastes the time away in miscellaneous trivialities, and the central theme of his struggle for salvation falls so far into the background as to be almost forgotten. The trivialities are entertaining enough in themselves, and they stage well, but they are digressions from the unity of the action. Nevertheless, at the end of the play Marlowe notably improved on the structure of his source. The English Faust Book made Faustus' last despairing soliloquy come *before* his final farewell to his scholar friends, whereas Marlowe reversed the order. This change in position avoided anticlimax and gave the play one of the greatest endings in all English drama.

Hand in hand with such betterments in plot construction went Marlowe's much more profound and poetic realization of the central religious conflict. In the English Faust Book this had been expressed merely as frequent and naive moralizing addressed to the reader directly, warning him how wicked Faustus was and advising him to avoid a similar fate. This technique Marlowe retained only in the opening and closing choruses, which stand as solemn portals of entrance to and exit from the drama. For the rest, he usually preferred to keep this meaning deeply implicit in the whole course of the plot, and when he brought it to the surface he gave it a superb dramatic context in the speeches of Mephistophilis, the Old Man, and the Good and Evil Angels. The latter are Marlowe's additions, derived in the last analysis from his knowledge of the medieval morality plays. He probably wished them to be considered, for the purposes of his play, just as objectively real and external to Faustus as, say, Mephistophilis, but they serve also as vivid symbols of the internal warfare in the soul of Faustus. Everywhere the dramatist has elevated and amplified the traits of Faustus' character, given them new passion, higher poetic reach, closer relation to the

theme of his temptation and agony. For the differ-
ence in sheer poetry one cannot do better than compare Faustus' famous rhapsody to Helen of Troy
beginning "Was this the face that launched a thousand ships?" with the commonplace details of Helen's
physical beauty which are all that are offered by the
English Faust Book (chapters 45 and 55). Yet it is sig-
nificant that Marlowe followed his source in the
fundamental matter of interpreting Helen as a decoy
used by the devils to seduce Faustus from the path
of salvation. Examine in the same way the final soliloquy. Many of its ideas came to Marlowe straight out
of his source, but he transfigured them with a poet's
more poignant passion. He drew also upon a number
of Biblical texts and upon his theological training at
Cambridge for an understanding of what was to the
Renaissance the most dreadful of psychological conditions, the suffering of the human soul in its last
moments of despair before damnation. Not least, perhaps, he drew upon introspection into his own per-
plexities.

Into the architecture of his play, too, Marlowe
built more of contemporary thought and learning
than may be visible at first glance. As recent scholarship has discovered, the dialogue on astronomy between Mephistophilis and Faustus in Scene VI pic-
tures not the then orthodox world system of Ptolemy
and Aristotle but a somewhat radical departure from
it proposed by Agostino Ricci, an Italian scientist, in
1513. Ricci retained the geocentric theory but denied
the existence of fiery and crystalline spheres rotating
around the earth, since these were not perceptible to
the senses. Writing at a time when the new helio-
centric theory of Copernicus was not yet widely
known in England, Marlowe was attracted to Ricci's

innovations by his own natural bent toward search-
ing and iconoclastic thought.

In the fields of witchcraft and theology there is
plenty of reason to think that Marlowe personally
was equally a rebel and sceptic, but he treated them
in an orthodox light in *Faustus,* for reasons which
will presently be discussed. Thus the play presents
as true the current Elizabethan beliefs that aspira-
tion for illicit knowledge and power might lead the
ambitious mind into black magic, that wonders
might then be done through the agency of demons,
and that such intercourse, if unrepented, would
surely bring on damnation. In passage after passage
portraying Faustus' dreams of magic, his incantations and remorse, and his whole behavior as a nec-
romancer Marlowe culled details from the vast
contemporary literature on witchcraft, in which
these subjects were systematically discussed. To be
sure, he refined somewhat the crasser popular su-
perstitions. For example, Mephistophilis is made to
say that not the words of Faustus' incantation but the
desire to win Faustus' soul summoned him from
the deep. And hell becomes for him less a place of
fire and brimstone than a lonely separation from God.
But both these ideas had often been voiced by the
better theologians of the age. What is new is Marlowe's heightening of them into magnificent poetry.

In a theological sense, the basic doctrine of the
play is that Faustus is at all times free both to resist
the temptation to evil and to repent after he has
fallen. This holds true even after he has signed the
contract selling his soul, even during the hour of
the last soliloquy, and up to the moment when the
clock strikes twelve. He could repent if he would accept the grace which God always offers him, as the

Old Man sees in his vision. But Faustus, unlike
the Old Man, does not believe strongly enough in
God's mercy and protection. He, who in the early
scenes took so much pride in being resolute in defy-
ing God, is not, ironically enough, sufficiently resolute to defy the devils when he wishes and needs to
do so. Hence he despairs and is lost. At times he
reaches for repentance but achieves only remorse,
which is regret not wholly committed to a plea for
forgiveness. All this doctrine, though not in the
learned yet poignant form given it by Marlowe, un-
derlies also the account in the English Faust Book.
And it has ample precedent in the non-Calvinistic
Protestantism of Marlowe's day.

   This theology in the play poses an interesting bio-
graphical problem since it is quite the opposite of
what all the surviving evidence indicates as to Marlowe's own convictions about Christianity. Robert
Greene, Richard Baines, Thomas Kyd and other con-
temporaries who knew Marlowe were unanimous in
saying that he became a blasphemous scoffer at the
religion in which he had been brought up. In the face
of their mutually corroborated testimony and the
absence of anything definite to the contrary, it is
hard to see Marlowe as other than a bitter enemy of
the Christian faith. This view is borne out also by
many strands of thought in *Tamburlaine* and *The
Jew of Malta.* The question is perhaps somewhat
complicated by the mystery which still hides the
nature of Marlowe's services for the Government and
the sinister circumstances of his death. If he was a
spy, if he was assassinated for political reasons, these
facts may conceivably have some sort of connection
with the anti-Christian ideas he uttered. The connection, however, seems slight and not likely to change

the conclusion that when Marlowe went about London scorning the Bible and defaming Christ he
meant what he said.

How, then, can his personal irreligion be recon-
ciled with the more or less orthodox theology of
Faustus? Perhaps by remembering that a dramatist
does not necessarily sponsor as his own the ideas
which his drama parades on the public stage in an
age of religious intolerance. But the problem goes
deeper. Marlowe's other dramas tend to be indirect
yet highly subjective expressions of his own grandi-
ose aspirations and defeats. Tamburlaine, Faustus,
Barabas, Gaveston, the Duke of Guise are so much
alike in their gigantic longings after unpermitted ends
as to seem only projections of one man, one spirit,
and that one is Christopher Marlowe. Faustus is
in some sense Marlowe. The truth may be that for all
his overt and ostentatious gibing at Christianity Marlowe sometimes experienced a dark hour when he
was overwhelmed by fear of his own apostasy and by
need for the love of God. Or perhaps it is best to say
that these feelings were latent in him but available
at the call of his poetic inspiration. *Faustus* is in part
the dramatic record of such an hour or of such buried
terrors. Hence Faustus' dreams of knowledge and
power, which were those of Marlowe; hence his
blaspheming, his sense of the loss of God, his agon-
ized despair. These are, after all, the gist of the play,
almost the entire play. The other people in the action
have virtually no character, and no function save to
help Faustus towards good or evil. To be sure, the
comic scenes afford welcome relief from the tautness
of the march of the main theme and even, by their
contrasting parody, a kind of second accentuation of
it. Essentially, though, it can be said truly that the

play deals with only one man and only one theme: Faustus, who gained the pleasures of the whole world and lost his soul. Its uniqueness as a tragedy emerges most clearly when we remember that it was written when Elizabethan drama was still young, and before the plays of Shakespeare. *Faustus*, the first of the major Elizabethan tragedies, was nothing short of an artistic revolution in its day.

THE PRINCIPAL DATES IN MARLOWE'S LIFE

1564 (Feb. 26) Christopher Marlowe born in Canterbury, one of nine children of John Marlowe and Catherine Arthur.

1579 (Jan. 14) Marlowe received a scholarship at King's School in Canterbury.

1580 (Autumn) Entered Corpus Christi College, Cambridge, being elected soon afterwards to a scholarship on the Archbishop Parker foundation.

1584 (Spring) Awarded the B. A. degree and continued his studies towards the M. A. but with extensive periods of absence during 1585 and 1586.

1587 (June 29) The Queen's Privy Council wrote to the Cambridge authorities stating that rumors of Marlowe's having gone abroad to join the Catholics should be silenced as false and that, on the contrary, he had been "employed in matters touching the benefit of his country."

1587 (July) Marlowe was awarded the M. A. degree by Cambridge. In this year Part I of *Tamburlaine* was staged by the Lord Admiral's Men, who likewise staged Part II either late in 1587 or in 1588.

1588   *Doctor Faustus* probably written. Staged presumably by the Lord Admiral's Men.

1589   (Sept. 18) Marlowe and William Bradley fought with rapiers in Hoglane in the London suburbs. Thomas Watson, poet and friend of Marlowe, intervened, was attacked by Bradley, and killed him. Marlowe and Watson imprisoned in Newgate.

(Sept. 19) Coroner's jury found that Watson acted in self-defense.

(Oct. 1) Marlowe released from prison on bail.

(Dec. 3) Watson and Marlowe freed of all charges after a court hearing.

1589-91   *The Jew of Malta, Edward II,* and *The Massacre at Paris* written and staged probably in that order during these years, but precise dates unknown.

1590   First edition of *Tamburlaine,* Part I, printed.

1592   First edition of *Tamburlaine,* Part II, printed.

1593   (May 12) Thomas Kyd, the dramatist, accused Marlowe of blasphemy and atheism.

(May 18) Marlowe summoned by the Privy Council to answer these charges. Similar charges filed against him by one Richard Baines at about this time.

(May 30) Marlowe spent the day at the inn at Deptford near London. Was stabbed to death by Ingram Frizer, who contended that Marlowe attacked him first in a quarrel over the bill.

(June 1) Coroner's jury found that Frizer acted in self-defense, and he received the Queen's pardon on June 28.

1594 First editions of Marlowe's *Dido* and *Edward II* published.

First edition of *The Massacre at Paris* also appeared soon afterwards.

1598 Marlowe's unfinished poem, *Hero and Leander,* completed and published by George Chapman.

1599 Marlowe's translation of Ovid's *Elegies,* published at some unknown time before this year, called in and burned by the censors in London.

1600 His translation of Lucan's *Pharsalia,* Book I, published.

1604 First extant edition of *Doctor Faustus* published.

1616 A considerably different text of the same play published, including new verse and prose scenes added by Rowley and Birde.

1633 First edition of *The Jew of Malta* published.

DRAMATIS PERSONAE

JOHN FAUSTUS, doctor of theology
MEPHISTOPHILIS, a lord of devils
VALDES } magicians
CORNELIUS }
Three SCHOLARS, friends to Faustus
OLD MAN

THE POPE
CARDINAL OF LORRAINE
CHARLES V, Emperor of Germany
KNIGHT
DUKE OF VANHOLT
DUCHESS OF VANHOLT

GOOD ANGEL
EVIL ANGEL
LUCIFER
BELZEBUB
SEVEN DEADLY SINS
ALEXANDER THE GREAT }
PARAMOUR OF ALEXANDER } Spirits
HELEN OF TROY }

WAGNER, servant to Faustus
CLOWN
ROBIN, the ostler
RALPH, a servingman
VINTNER
HORSE-COURSER

CHORUS

Friars, Devils, Attendants

DOCTOR FAUSTUS

❧

Enter Chorus.

CHORUS. Not marching now in fields of Thrasy-
    mene
Where Mars did mate the Carthaginians,
Nor sporting in the dalliance of love
In courts of kings where state is overturned,
Nor in the pomp of proud audacious deeds
Intends our Muse to daunt his heavenly verse:
Only this, Gentlemen, we must perform,
The form of Faustus' fortunes good or bad.
To patient judgments we appeal our plaud
And speak for Faustus in his infancy.   10
Now is he born, his parents base of stock,
In Germany within a town called Rhodes;
Of riper years to Wittenberg he went
Whereas his kinsmen chiefly brought him up;
So soon he profits in divinity,
The fruitful plot of scholarism graced,
That shortly he was graced with Doctor's name,
Excelling all whose sweet delight disputes
In heavenly matters of theology,
Till swollen with cunning, of a self-conceit,   20

1 **Thrasymene** Lake Trasimene, where Carthaginians defeat-
ed Romans, 217 B.C. 2 **mate** ally himself with 4 **state** political power 6 **daunt** demean 9 **our plaud** for our applause 12
Rhodes Roda in the Duchy of Saxe-Altenburg 13 **Wittenberg**
university in Saxony 14 **Whereas** where 16 **scholarism** scholarship 17 **graced** adorned; pun on entry of candidate's name
in university Grace Book, permitting him to get his degree
18 **delight disputes** delight is to dispute 20 **cunning learning
of a self-conceit** out of pride

His waxen wings did mount above his reach
And melting heavens conspired his overthrow.
For, falling to a devilish exercise
And glutted more with learning's golden gifts,
He surfeits upon cursed necromancy.
Nothing so sweet as magic is to him,
Which he prefers before his chiefest bliss—
And this the man that in his study sits.   *Exit.*

Scene I

❧

Enter Faustus in his Study.

FAUSTUS. Settle thy studies, Faustus, and begin
To sound the depth of that thou wilt profess.
Having commenced, be a divine in show,
Yet level at the end of every art
And live and die in Aristotle's works:
Sweet Analytics, 'tis thou hast ravished me! [*Reads.*]
Bene disserere est finis logicis—
Is to dispute well logic's chiefest end?
Affords this art no greater miracle?
10 Then read no more; thou hast attained the end.
A greater subject fitteth Faustus' wit:

21 **waxen wings** allusion to the wings of Icarus fastened to his
body by wax which melted when he flew too near the sun 22
melting heavens heat of the sun 25 **necromancy** black magic,
especially the art of summoning the dead 27 **chiefest bliss**
salvation of his soul 1 **Settle thy studies** decide your future
course of study 2 **profess** teach or practise 3 **commenced**
graduated 4 **level** aim 6 **Analytics** Aristotle's *Prior Analytics*
and *Posterior Analytics,* works on logic

Bid ὂν καὶ υὴ ὂν farewell, Galen come,
Seeing *ubi desinit philosophus, ibi incipit medicus;*
Be a physician, Faustus, heap up gold
And be eternized for some wondrous cure.   [*Reads.*]
Summum bonum medicinae sanitas—
The end of physic is our bodies' health:
Why, Faustus, hast thou not attained that end?
Is not thy common talk sound aphorisms?
Are not thy bills hung up as monuments   20
Whereby whole cities have escaped the plague
And thousand desperate maladies been eased?
Yet art thou still but Faustus, and a man.
Couldst thou make men to live eternally
Or, being dead, raise them to life again,
Then this profession were to be esteemed.
Physic, farewell. Where is Justinian?   [*Reads.*]
Si una eademque res legatur duobus,
Alter rem, alter valorem rei, etc.—
A pretty case of paltry legacies!   30
Exhaereditare filium non potest pater nisi—
Such is the subject of the Institute
And universal body of the law.
His study fits a mercenary drudge
Who aims at nothing but external trash,
Too servile and illiberal for me.
When all is done, divinity is best.

12 ὂν καὶ μὴ ὂν being and not being, according to Aristotle
Galen Greek authority on medicine in the second century A.D.
13 **ubi desinit** . . . where the philosopher stops the physician
begins 15 **eternized** eternally famous 19 **aphorisms** concise
statements of medical truths 20 **bills** prescriptions 27 **Justinian**
Emperor who codified Roman law in the sixth century A.D.
28 **Si una** . . . If one and the same thing is bequeathed to two
persons, one shall have the thing itself, the other its equivalent
in value, etc. 31 **Exhaereditare** . . . A father cannot disinherit
his son unless—32 **Institute** title of one of Justinian's codifica-
tions 35 **external trash** property

Jerome's Bible, Faustus, view it well: [*Reads.*]
Stipendium peccati mors est—Ha! *Stipendium, etc.*
40 The reward of sin is death. That's hard.
*Si pecasse negamus, fallimur, et nulla est in nobis
    veritas—*
If we say that we have no sin
We deceive ourselves, and there's no truth in us.
Why then belike
We must sin and so consequently die,
Ay, we must die an everlasting death.
What doctrine call you this, *Che sera, sera:*
What will be, shall be? Divinity, adieu!
These metaphysics of magicians
50 And necromantic books are heavenly:
Lines, circles, signs, letters and characters—
Ay, these are those that Faustus most desires.
O what a world of profit and delight,
Of power, of honor, of omnipotence,
Is promised to the studious artisan!
All things that move between the quiet poles
Shall be at my command. Emperors and kings
Are but obeyed in their several provinces,
Nor can they raise the wind or rend the clouds;
60 But his dominion that exceeds in this
Stretcheth as far as doth the mind of man.
A sound magician is a mighty god:
Here, Faustus, try thy brains to gain a deity!

Enter WAGNER.

Wagner, commend me to my dearest friends,

38 **Jerome's Bible** Latin Bible known as the Vulgate, prepared
by St. Jerome 392-404 A.D.   47 **Che sera, sera** what is fated to
happen will happen   49 **metaphysics** basic principles   51 **signs**
symbols of the signs or twelve equal parts into which the
zodiac was divided   56 **quiet poles** motionless poles of the cosmos upon whose axis were supposed to roll the spheres of stars
and planets   60 **exceeds** excels

The German Valdes and Cornelius;
Request them earnestly to visit me.

    WAGNER. I will, sir.   *Exit.*

    FAUST. Their conference will be a greater help to
    me

Than all my labors, plod I ne'er so fast.

    Enter the GOOD ANGEL *and the* EVIL ANGEL.

    G. ANG. O Faustus, lay that damned book aside   70
And gaze not on it, lest it tempt thy soul
And heap God's heavy wrath upon thy head.
Read, read the Scriptures! That is blasphemy.

    E. ANG. Go forward, Faustus, in that famous art
Wherein all nature's treasury in contained:
Be thou on earth, as Jove is in the sky,
Lord and commander of these elements.

                           Exeunt ANGELS.

    FAUST. How am I glutted with conceit of this!
Shall I make spirits fetch me what I please,
Resolve me of all ambiguities,   80
Perform what desperate enterprise I will?
I'll have them fly to India for gold,
Ransack the océan for orient pearl,
And search all corners of the new-found world
For pleasant fruits and princely delicates;
I'll have them read me strange philosophy
And tell the secrets of all foreign kings;
I'll have them wall all Germany with brass
And make swift Rhine circle fair Wittenberg;
I'll have them fill the public schools with silk   90
Wherewith the students shall be bravely clad;

76 **Jove** God 77 **elements** the earth, together with the orbs
of water, air, and fire surrounding it 78 **glutted with conceit**
filled with the idea 81 **desperate** impossibly difficult 83 **orient**
glowing 84 **new-found world** America 90 **public schools** university classrooms

I'll levy soldiers with the coin they bring,
And chase the Prince of Parma from our land
And reign sole king of all our provinces;
Yea, stranger engines for the brunt of war
Than was the fiery keel at Antwerp's bridge
I'll make my servile spirits to invent!

Enter VALDES *and* CORNELIUS.

Come, German Valdes and Cornelius,
And make me blest with your sage conference.
100 Valdes, sweet Valdes and Cornelius,
Know that your words have won me at the last
To practise magic and concealéd arts;
Yet not your words only, but mine own fantasy
That will receive no object for my head
But ruminates on necromantic skill.
Philosophy is odious and obscure,
Both law and physic are for petty wits,
Divinity is basest of the three,
Unpleasant, harsh, contemptible and vile;
110 'Tis magic, magic, that hath ravished me!
Then, gentle friends, aid me in this attempt,
And I that have with concise syllogisms
Gravelled the pastors of the German church,
And made the flowering pride of Wittenberg
Swarm to my problems as the infernal spirits
On sweet Musaeus when he came to hell,

93 **Prince of Parma** governor-general of the Spanish rule in the Netherlands 95 **engines** mechanical inventions **brunt** heat 96 **fiery keel . . .** burning ship used to break through Parma's bridge across the Scheldt during the siege of Antwerp, 1585 103 **fantasy** imagination 104 **receive no object** think of nothing else 107 **wits** minds 113 **gravelled** silenced 114 **flowering pride** best students 115 **problems** mathematical and logical lectures 116 **Musaeus** mythical poet mentioned in Virgil's *Aeneid*

Will be as cunning as Agrippa was
Whose shadows made all Europe honor him.
   VALD. Faustus, these books, thy wit and our expe-
      rience
Shall make all nations to canonize us.   120
As Indian Moors obey their Spanish lords
So shall the subjects of every element
Be always serviceable to us three:
Like lions shall they guard us when we please,
Like Almain rutters with their horsemen's staves,
Or Lapland giants trotting by our sides;
Sometimes like women, or unwedded maids,
Shadowing more beauty in their airy brows
Than has the white breasts of the queen of love;
From Venice shall they drag huge argosies   130
And from America the golden fleece
That yearly stuffs old Philip's treasury,
If learned Faustus will be resolute.
   FAUST. Valdes, as resolute am I in this
As thou to live; therefore object it not.
   CORN. The miracles that magic will perform
Will make thee vow to study nothing else.
He that is grounded in astrology,
Enriched with tongues, well seen in minerals,
Hath all the principles magic doth require.   140
Then doubt not, Faustus, but to be renowned
And more frequented for this mystery

117 **Agrippa** Henry Cornelius Agrippa von Nettesheim,
early sixteenth-century scholar reputed to be a magician
118 **shadows** shades raised from the dead by magic 120 **canonize** accept as saints 121 **Indian Moors** dark American In-
dians 122 **subjects** spirits inhabiting each of the four elements
125 **Almain rutters** German horsemen **staves** lance shafts
129 **queen of love** Venus 130 **argosies** rich merchant ships
131 **golden fleece** gold from the American mines carried to
Spain in the annual plate-fleet 132 **Philip** Philip II of Spain
135 **object it not** make no such objection 139 **well seen** expert

Than heretofore the Delphian oracle.
The spirits tell me they can dry the sea
And fetch the treasure of all foreign wrecks—
Ay, all the wealth that our forefathers hid
Within the massy entrails of the earth.
Then tell me, Faustus, what shall we three want?

   FAUST. Nothing, Cornelius. O this cheers my soul!
150 Come, show me some demonstrations magical
That I may conjure in some lusty grove
And have these joys in full possessión.

   VALD. Then haste thee to some solitary grove
And bear wise Bacon's and Albanus' works,
The Hebrew Psalter and new Testament;
And whatsoever else is requisite
We will inform thee ere our conference cease.

   CORN. Valdes, first let him know the words of art,
And then, all other ceremonies learned,
160 Faustus may try his cunning by himself.

   VALD. First I'll instruct thee in the rudiments,
And then wilt thou be perfecter than I.

     FAUST. Then come and dine with me, and after
     meat
We'll canvas every quiddity thereof;
For ere I sleep I'll try what I can do:
This night I'll conjure though I die therefore.

                      Exeunt.

147 **massy** massive 151 **lusty** thick 154 **Bacon** Roger Bacon, 1214-94, English scientist famed as a magician **Albanus** perhaps Pietro d'Albano, thirteenth-century alchemist 155 **Hebrew Psalter** Old Testament psalms in Hebrew 164 **canvas** explore **quiddity** essential part

Scene II

✿

Enter two SCHOLARS.

1 SCHOLAR. I wonder what's become of Faustus, that was wont to make our schools ring with *sic probo*?

2 SCH. That shall we know, for see here comes his boy.

Enter WAGNER [*carrying wine.*]

1 SCH. How now, sirrah; where's thy master?

WAG. God in heaven knows.

2 SCH. Why, dost not thou know?

WAG. Yes, I know; but that follows not.

1 SCH. Go to, sirrah; leave your jesting and tell us 10 where he is.

WAG. That follows not necessary by force of argument that you, being licentiate, should stand upon it; therefore acknowledge your error and be attentive.

2 SCH. Why, didst thou not say thou knewest?

1 SCH. Yes, sirrah, I heard you.

WAG. Ask my fellow if I be a thief.

2 SCH. Well, you will not tell us?

WAG. Yes, sir, I will tell you. Yet if you were not dunces you would never ask me such a question, for 20 is not he *corpus naturale*, and is not that *mobile*?

2 **sic probo** thus I prove (a formula in scholastic disputations) 9 **follows not** is not a logical conclusion 13 **licentiate** admitted to candidacy for a Master's or Doctor's degree **stand rely** 17 **Ask my fellow** . . . proverb meaning that the witness is biased 21 **corpus naturale** natural body capable of being moved

Then wherefore should you ask me such a question?
But that I am by nature phlegmatic, slow to wrath
and prone to lechery (to love, I would say), it were
not for you to come within forty foot of the place of
execution, although I do not doubt to see you both
hanged the next sessions. Thus having triumphed
over you, I will set my countenance like a precisian,
and begin to speak thus: Truly, my dear brethren,
30 my master is within at dinner with Valdes and Cornelius, as this wine, if it could speak, would inform
your worships; and so the Lord bless you, preserve
you, and keep you, my dear brethren, my dear
brethren.   *Exit.*

1 SCH. Nay, then I fear he is fallen into that damned
art for which they two are infamous through the
world.

2 SCH. Were he a stranger and not allied to me, yet
should I grieve for him. But come, let us go and in-
40 form the Rector, and see if he by his grave counsel
can reclaim him.

1 SCH. O but I fear me nothing can reclaim him.

2 SCH. Yet let us try what we can do.   *Exeunt.*

25 **place of execution** dining room   27 **sessions** court sessions
28 **precision** Puritan   40 **Rector** president of the university

Scene III

❧

Enter FAUSTUS *to conjure.*

FAUST. Now that the gloomy shadow of the earth,
Longing to view Orion's drizzling look,
Leaps from the antarctic world unto the sky
And dims the welkin with her pitchy breath,
Faustus, begin thine incantations
And try if devils will obey thy hest,
Seeing thou has prayed and sacrificed to them.
Within this circle is Jehovah's name

[*He draws the circle on the ground.*]

Forward and backward anagrammatized,
The breviated names of holy saints,   10
Figures of every adjunct to the heavens
And characters of signs and erring stars,
By which the spirits are enforced to rise.
Then fear not, Faustus, but be resolute
And try the uttermost magic can perform. [*Thunder.*]
Sint mihi dei Acherontis propitii! Valeat numen tri-
        plex Iehovae!
Ignei aerii aquatici spiritus, salvete! Orientis princeps
Belzebub, inferni ardentis monarcha, et Demogor-

2 **Orion** a winter constellation, supposed to bring storms 3
antarctic world southern hemisphere 4 **welkin** heavens 6 **hest**
behest 9 **anagrammatized** letters of the mystic Hebrew name
for God transposed in different ways so as to spell other names
for God, all of them potent in magic 10 **breviated** abbreviated
11 **adjunct** heavenly body 12 **characters** . . . symbols of the
signs of the Zodiac **erring stars** planets 16-21 **Sint** . . . Favor
me, you gods of Acheron! Yield to the triune power of Jehovah! (inscribed in the circle) Hail, likewise, you spirits of
fire, air and water! Belzebub, prince of the east, monarch of

20 *gon, propitiamus vos, ut appareat et surgat Meph-*
   istophilis!

> [FAUSTUS *pauses. Thunder still.*]

Quid tu moraris? Per Iehovam, Gehennam et conse-
   cratam aquam quam nunc spargo, signumque
   crucis quod nunc facio, et per vota nostra, ipse
   nunc surgat nobis dicatus Mephistophilis!

> [MEPHISTOPHILIS *in the shape of a dragon*
> *rises from the earth outside the circle.*]

I charge thee to return and change thy shape;
Thou art too ugly to attend on me.
Go, and return an old Franciscan friar;
That holy shape becomes a devil best.   *Exit* MEPH.
30 I see there's virtue in my heavenly words:
Who would not be proficient in this art?
How pliant is this Mephistophilis,
Full of obedience and humility!
Such is the force of magic and my spells.
Now, Faustus, thou art conjuror laureate
That canst command great Mephistophilis:
Quin redis, Mephistophilis, fratris imagine!

> *Re-enter* MEPHISTOPHILIS *like a Friar.*

MEPH. Now, Faustus, what wouldst thou have me
do?
40   FAUST. I charge thee wait upon me whilst I live
To do whatever Faustus shall command,

blazing hell, and Demogorgon, we invoke your favor in order
that Mephistophilis may appear and ascend 22-32 **Quid**
. . . Why do you delay? By Jehovah, by Gehenna, and by the
holy water which now I sprinkle, by the sign of the cross
which now I make, and by the prayers I have offered you,
send at my command none other than Mephistophilis! 30
virtue power; ironic pun on moral virtue 35 **laureate** crowned
with laurel, triumphant 37 **Quin** . . . Return, Mephistophilis,
in the likeness of a friar

Be it be make the moon drop from her sphere
Or the ocean to overwhelm the world.

MEPH. I am a servant to great Lucifer
And may not follow thee without his leave:
No more than he commands must we perform.

FAUST. Did not he charge thee to appear to me?

MEPH. No, I came now hither of my own accord.

FAUST. Did not my conjuring speeches raise thee?
Speak!   50

MEPH. That was the cause, but yet *per accidens,*
For when we hear one rack the name of God,
Abjure the Scriptures and his Savior Christ,
We fly in hope to get his glorious soul;
Nor will we come unless he use such means
Whereby he is in danger to be damned;
Therefore the shortest cut for conjuring
Is stoutly to abjure the Trinity
And pray devoutly to the prince of hell.

FAUST. So Faustus hath   60
Already done, and holds this principle,
There is no chief but only Belzebub
To whom Faustus doth dedicate himself.
This word damnation terrifies not him
For he confounds hell in Elisium;
His ghost be with the old philosophers!
But leaving these vain trifles of men's souls—
Tell me what is that Lucifer thy lord?

MEPH. Arch-regent and commander of all spirits.

FAUST. Was not that Lucifer an angel once?   70

MEPH. Yes, Faustus, and most dearly loved of God.

FAUST. How comes it, then, that he is prince of
devils?

MEPH. O by aspiring pride and insolence

Faustus he has thinks - but he power - is powerless

51 **per accidens** indirectly, aside from any compulsion in the
conjuring itself 52 **rack** torture 65 **confounds** . . . believes not
in hell but in Elisium, the pagan otherworld

For which God threw him from the face of heaven.
    FAUST. And what are you that live with Lucifer?
    MEPH. Unhappy spirits that fell with Lucifer,
Conspired against our God with Lucifer,
And are forever damned with Lucifer.
80   FAUST. Where are you damned?
    MEPH. In hell.
    FAUST. How comes it, then, that thou art out of
hell?
    MEPH. Why, this is hell, nor am I out of it:
Thinkst thou that I who saw the face of God
And tasted the eternal joys of heaven
Am not tormented with ten thousand hells
In being deprived of everlasting bliss?
O Faustus, leave these frivolous demands
90 Which strike a terror to my fainting soul!
    FAUST. What, is great Mephistophilis so passionate
For being deprivéd of the joys of heaven?
Learn thou of Faustus manly fortitude
And scorn those joys thou never shalt possess.
Go, bear these tidings to great Lucifer:
Seeing Faustus hath incurred eternal death
By desperate thoughts against Jove's deity,
Say he surrenders up to him his soul
So he will spare him four-and-twenty years,
100 Letting him live in all voluptuousness,
Having thee ever to attend on me:
To give me whatsoever I shall ask,
To tell me whatsoever I demand,
To slay mine enemies and aid my friends,
And always be obedient to my will.
Go, and return to mighty Lucifer,
And meet me in my study at midnight
And then resolve me of thy master's mind.

89 **demands** questions 91 **passionate** grieved 108 **resolve in-**
form

MEPH. I will, Faustus.   *Exit.*

FAUST. Had I as many souls as there be stars   110
I'd give them all for Mephistophilis!
By him I'll be great Emperor of the world,
And make a bridge thorough the moving air
To pass the ocean with a band of men;
I'll join the hills that bind the Afric shore
And make that country continent to Spain,
And both contributory to my crown;
The Emperor shall not live but by my leave,
Nor any potentate of Germany.
Now that I have obtained what I desire   120
I'll live in speculation of this art
Till Mephistophilis return again.   *Exit.*

Scene IV

❧

Enter WAGNER *and the* CLOWN.

WAG. Sirrah boy, come hither.

CLOWN. How, boy? Swowns, boy! I hope you have
seen many boys with such pickadevaunts as I have.
Boy, quotha!

WAG. Tell me, sirrah, hast thou any comings in?

CLOWN. Ay, and goings out too; you may see else.

WAG. Alas, poor slave. See how poverty jesteth in
his nakedness: the villain is bare and out of service,

113 **thorough** through 115 **hills that bind** . . . hills on either
side of the Straits of Gibraltar which, when joined, would
unite Africa and Europe as one continent 117 **contributory**
subject 121 **speculation** study 2 **Swowns** by God's wounds
3 **pickadevaunts** pointed beards **quotha** indeed 5 **comings in**
income 8 **out of service** unemployed

and so hungry that I know he would give his soul
10 to the Devil for a shoulder of mutton, though it were
blood-raw.

CLOWN. How, my soul to the Devil for a shoulder
of mutton though it were blood raw? Not so, good
friend: by'r Lady, I had need have it well roasted,
and good sauce to it, if I pay so dear.

WAG. Well, wilt thou serve me, and I'll make thee
go like *Qui mihi discipulus?*

CLOWN. How, in verse?

WAG. No, sirrah, in beaten silk and stavesacre.
20   CLOWN. How, how: knave's acre? Ay, I thought
that was all the land his father left him. Do ye hear.
I would be sorry to rob you of your living.

WAG. Sirrah, I say in stavesacre.

CLOWN. Oho, oho: stavesacre! Why then, belike,
if I were your man I should be full of vermin.

WAG. So thou shalt, whether thou beest with me or
no. But sirrah, leave your jesting, and bind yourself
presently unto me for seven years, or I'll turn all the
lice about thee into familiars, and they shall tear thee
30 in pieces.

CLOWN. Do you hear, sir? You may save that labor;
they are too familiar with me already. Swowns, they
are as bold with my flesh, as if they had paid for my
meat and drink.

WAG. Well, do you hear, sirrah: hold, take these
guilders.   [*Gives money.*]

CLOWN. Gridirons—what be they?

WAG. Why, French crowns.

17 **go** be dressed **Qui** . . . my pupil (quotation from a Latin
verse) 19 **beaten silk** silk with metal embroidery **stavesacre** a
fabric; also an ointment for killing lice 20 **knave's acre** name
of a dingy lane in London; also any land owned by a knave 27
bind sign servant's papers 29 **familiars** attendant demons
36 **guilders** Dutch florins 38 **French crowns** French coin often
counterfeited or debased; also baldness due to venereal disease

CLOWN. Mass, but for the name of French crowns a man were as good have as many English counters. 40 And what should I do with these?

WAG. Why now, sirrah, thou art at an hour's warning whensoever or wheresoever the devil shall fetch thee.

CLOWN. No, no! Here, take your gridirons again.

WAG. Truly, I'll none of them.

CLOWN. Truly, but you shall.

WAG. Bear witness, I gave them him.

CLOWN. Bear witness, I give them you again.

WAG. Well, I will cause two devils presently to 50 fetch thee away. Baliol and Belcher!   [Conjures.]

CLOWN. Let your Belly-oh and your Belcher come here, and I'll knock them, they were never so knocked since they were devils. Say I should kill one of them, what would folks say: do ye see yonder tall fellow in the round slop? He has killed the devil! So I should be called kill-devil all the parish over.

Enter two DEVILS, *and the* CLOWN *runs up and down crying.*

WAG. Baliol and Belcher! Spirits away!
                              Exeunt [DEVILS.]

CLOWN. What, are they gone? A vengeance on them, they have vile long nails! There was a he-devil, 60 and a she-devil. I'll tell you how you may know them: all he-devils has horns, and all she-devils has clifts and cloven feet.

WAG. Well, sirrah, follow me.

CLOWN. But do you hear, if I should serve you,

39 **Mass** by the mass 40 **English counters** worthless tokens used by merchants in counting money; also name of an English jail 42 **warning** notice 51 **Baliol** Belial, punning on Belly-all, and Belcher 56 **round slop** wide pants 62 **clifts** clefts

would you teach me to raise up Banios and Bel-
cheos?

WAG. I will teach thee to turn thyself to anything—
to a dog, or a cat, or a mouse, or a rat, or any thing.

70   CLOWN. How? a Christian fellow to a dog or a cat,
a mouse or a rat? No, no, sir! If you turn me into any
thing, let it be in the likeness of a little pretty frisk-
ing flea, that I may be here and there and everywhere. O I'll tickle the pretty wenches' plackets, I'll
be amongst them, i'faith!

WAG. Well, sirrah, come.

CLOWN. But do you hear, Wagner?

WAG. How? Baliol and Belcher!

CLOWN. O Lord, I pray sir, let Banio and Belcher
80   go sleep.

WAG. Villain, call me Master Wagner, and let thy
left eye be diametarily fixt upon my right heel with
quasi vestigias nostras insistere.   *Exit.*

CLOWN. God forgive me, he speaks Dutch fustian.
Well, I'll follow him, I'll serve him; that's flat.   *Exit.*

Scene V

❧

Enter FAUSTUS *in his Study.*

FAUST. Now, Faustus, must thou needs be damned
And canst thou not be saved.
What boots it, then, to think of God or heaven?
Away with such vain fancies, and despair—

66 **Banio** pun on bagnio, a brothel 82 **diametarily** diametri-
cally 83 **quasi** . . . as if walking in my footsteps 84 **fustian**
nonsense 3 **boots** benefits

Despair in God and trust in Belzebub.
Now go not backward, no!
Faustus, be resolute: why waverest thou?
O something soundeth in mine ears:
"Abjure this magic, turn to God again!"
Ay, and Faustus will turn to God again.   10
To God? He loves thee not;
The God thou servest is thine own appetite,
Wherein is fixed the love of Belzebub.
To him I'll build an altar and a church
And offer lukewarm blood of newborn babes.

Enter GOOD ANGEL *and* EVIL ANGEL.

G. ANG. Sweet Faustus, leave that execrable art.

E. ANG. Go forward, Faustus, in that famous art.

FAUST. Contrition, prayer, repentance—what of them?

G. ANG. O they are means to bring thee unto heaven!

E. ANG. Rather illusions, fruits of lunacy,
That makes men foolish that do trust them most.

G. ANG. Sweet Faustus, think of heaven and heavenly things.

E. ANG. No, Faustus, think of honor and of wealth.
                              [*Exeunt* ANGELS.]

FAUST. Of wealth!
Why, the signiory of Emden shall be mine.
When Mephistophilis shall stand by me
What God can hurt me? Faustus, thou art safe;   30
Cast no more doubts. Come, Mephistophilis,
And bring glad tidings from great Lucifer.
Is't not midnight? Come, Mephistophilis!
Veni, veni, Mephistophile!

28 **signiory** domain **Emden** chief port of the principality of
East-Friesland 31 **Cast** reckon 34 **Veni . . . Come!** Come,
Mephistophilis!

Enter MEPHISTOPHILIS.

Now tell me what says Lucifer, thy lord?

MEPH. That I shall wait on Faustus whilst I live,
So he will buy my service with his soul.

FAUST. Already Faustus hath hazarded that for thee.

40 MEPH. But, Faustus, thou must bequeath it solemnly
And write a deed of gift with thine own blood,
For that security craves great Lucifer.
If thou deny it, I will back to hell.

FAUST. Stay, Mephistophilis, and tell me what good
Will my soul do thy lord?

MEPH. Enlarge his kingdom.

FAUST. Is that the reason why he tempts us thus?

MEPH. *Solamen miseris socios habuisse doloris.*

FAUST. Why, have you any pain that tortures others?

50 MEPH. As great as have the human souls of men.
But tell me, Faustus, shall I have thy soul?
And I will be thy slave, and wait on thee,
And tell thee more than thou hast wit to ask.

FAUST. Ay, Mephistophilis, I give it thee.

MEPH. Then, Faustus, stab thine arm courageously,
And bind thy soul that at some certain day
Great Lucifer may claim it as his own,
And then be thou as great as Lucifer.

FAUST. Lo, Mephistophilis, for love of thee
[*Stabbing his arm.*]
60 I cut mine arm, and with my proper blood
Assure my soul to be great Lucifer's.
Chief lord and regent of perpetual night,

47 **Solamen** . . . Misery loves company   60 **proper** own

View here the blood that trickles from mine arm
And let it be propitious for my wish!
     MEPH. But, Faustus, thou must
Write it in manner of a deed of gift.
     FAUST. Ay, so I will. [*Writes.*] But, Mephistophilis,
My blood congeals and I can write no more.
     MEPH. I'll fetch thee fire to dissolve it straight.

Exit.

     FAUST. What might the staying of my blood por- 70
     tend?
Is it unwilling I should write this bill?
Why streams it not, that I may write afresh?
"Faustus gives to thee his soul"—ah, there it stayed.
Why shouldst thou not? Is not thy soul thine own?
Then write again: "Faustus gives to thee his soul."

     Re-enter MEPHISTOPHILIS *with a chafer of coals.*

     MEPH. Here's fire; come, Faustus, set it on.
     FAUST. So: now the blood begins to clear again;
Now will I make an end immediately.   [*Writes.*]
     MEPH. [*Aside.*] O what will not I do to obtain his
soul!   80
     FAUST. *Consummatum est*—this bill is ended;
And Faustus hath bequeathed his soul to Lucifer.
But what is this inscription on mine arm?
"*Homo, fuge!*" Whither should I fly?
If unto God, he'll throw me down to hell.
My senses are deceived; here's nothing writ.
I see it plain: here in this place is writ
"*Homo, fuge!*" Yet shall not Faustus fly.
     MEPH. I'll fetch him somewhat to delight his mind.

Exit.

---

71 **bill** contract 76 **chafer** pan with burning coals underneath
81 **Consummatum est** it is finished 84 **Homo, fuge** Man, flee

Re-enter MEPHISTOPHILIS *with* DEVILS, *giving crowns
and rich apparel to* FAUSTUS, *and dance, and then
depart.*

90   FAUST. Speak, Mephistophilis, what means this show?

MEPH. Nothing, Faustus, but to delight thy mind withal

And to show thee what magic can perform.

FAUST. But may I raise up spirits when I please?

MEPH. Ay, Faustus, and do greater things than these.

FAUST. Then there's enough for a thousand souls.

Here, Mephistophilis, receive this scroll,

A deed of gift of body and of soul;

100   But yet conditionally that thou perform

All articles prescribed between us both.

MEPH. Faustus, I swear by hell and Lucifer

To effect all promises between us made.

FAUST. Then hear me read them: [*Reads.*]

"On these conditions following:

First, that Faustus may be a spirit in form and substance.

Secondly, that Mephistophilis shall be his servant and at his command.

110   Thirdly, that Mephistophilis shall do for him, and bring him whatsoever.

Fourthly, that he shall be in his chamber or house invisible.

Lastly, that he shall appear to the said John Faustus at all times, in what form or shape soever he please.

I, John Faustus of Wittenberg, Doctor, by these presents do give both body and soul to Lucifer, Prince of the East, and his minister Mephistoph-

100 **conditionally** on condition that   101 **articles** stipulations

ilis, and furthermore grant unto them, that 24 120
years being expired, the articles above written
inviolate, full power to fetch or carry the said
John Faustus body and soul, flesh, blood, or
goods, into their habitation wheresoever.

　　　　　By me John Faustus."

MEPH. Speak, Faustus, do you deliver this as your
deed?

FAUST. Ay, take it, and the devil give thee good
on't.

MEPH. Now, Faustus, ask what thou wilt.

FAUST. First will I question with thee about hell.   130
Tell me, where is the place that men call hell?

MEPH. Under the heavens.

FAUST.　　　　　　　　　Ay, but whereabout?

MEPH. Within the bowels of these elements,
Where we are tortured and remain forever.
Hell hath no limits, nor is circumscribed
In one self place, for where we are is hell
And where hell is there must we ever be;
And, to conclude, when all the world dissolves
And every creature shall be purified,
All places shall be hell that is not heaven.   140

FAUST. Come, I think hell's a fable.

MEPH. Ay, think so, till experience change thy
mind.

FAUST. Why, thinkst thou then that Faustus shall
be damned?

MEPH. Ay, of necessity, for here's the scroll
Wherein thou hast given thy soul to Lucifer.

FAUST. Ay, and body too; but what of that?
Thinkst thou that Faustus is so fond to imagine

121-122 **articles . . . inviolate** the above conditions having
been kept 133 **these elements** all the four elements below the
moon's sphere 135 **circumscribed** bounded 136 **self** single
138 **dissolves** by fire at the Last Judgment 149 **fond** foolish

150 That after this life there is any pain?
Tush, these are trifles and mere old wives' tales.
    MEPH. But, Faustus, I am an instance to prove the
        contrary,
For I am damnéd, and am now in hell.
    FAUST. How, now in hell?
Nay, and this be hell I'll willingly be damned.
What, walking, disputing, etcetera?
But leaving off this, let me have a wife,
The fairest maid in Germany,
For I am wanton and lascivious
160 And cannot live without a wife.
    MEPH. How, a wife?
I prithee, Faustus, talk not of a wife.
    FAUST. Nay, sweet Mephistophilis, fetch me one,
for I will have one.
    MEPH. Well, thou wilt have one. Sit there till I
        come;
I'll fetch thee a wife in the devil's name.   [*Exit.*]

Re-enter MEPHISTOPHILIS *with a* DEVIL *dressed like a
woman, with fireworks.*

    MEPH. Tell me, Faustus, how dost thou like thy
wife?
    FAUST. A plague on her for a hot whore!
170   MEPH. Tut, Faustus,
Marriage is but a ceremonial toy.
If thou lovest me, think no more of it.
I'll cull thee out the fairest courtesans
And bring them every morning to thy bed;
She whom thine eye shall like thy heart shall have,
Be she as chaste as was Penelope,

155 **and** if 171 **ceremonial toy** trifling ceremony 173 **cull**
choose 176 **Penelope** faithful wife of Ulysses

As wise as Saba, or as beautiful
As was bright Lucifer before his fall. [*Exeunt.*]

Scene VI

Enter again FAUSTUS *and* MEPHISTOPHILIS.

MEPH. Hold, take this book: peruse it thoroughly.
The iterating of these lines brings gold,
The framing of this circle on the ground
Brings whirlwinds, tempests, thunder and lightning;
Pronounce this thrice devoutly to thyself
And men in armor shall appear to thee,
Ready to execute what thou desirest.

FAUST. Thanks, Mephistophilis, yet fain would I have a book wherein I might behold all spells and incantations, that I might raise up spirits when I please.

MEPH. Here they are in this book.

There turn to them.

FAUST. Now would I have a book where I might see all characters and planets of the heavens, that I might know their motions and dispositions.

MEPH. Here they are too. *Turn to them.*

FAUST. Nay, let me have one book more, and then I have done, wherein I might see all plants, herbs, and trees that grow upon the earth.

MEPH. Here they be.

FAUST. O thou art deceived!

177 Saba Queen of Sheba **2 iterating** repeating **14 characters and planets** symbols of the planets **15 dispositions** astrological effects

MEPH. Tut, I warrant thee. *Turn to them.*

FAUST. When I behold the heavens then I repent
And curse thee, wicked Mephistophilis,
Because thou hast deprived me of those joys.

MEPH. Why, thinkest thou heaven is such a glorious thing?
I tell thee, Faustus, 'tis not half so fair
As thou or any man that breathes on earth.

FAUST. How provest thou that?

30   MEPH. It was made for man; therefore is man more excellent.

FAUST. If it were made for man, 'twas made for me.
I will renounce this magic and repent.

Enter GOOD ANGEL *and* EVIL ANGEL.

G. ANGEL. Faustus, repent; yet God will pity thee.
E. ANGEL. Thou art a spirit; God cannot pity thee.
FAUST. Who buzzeth in mine ears I am a spirit?
Be I a devil yet God may pity me.
Ay, God will pity me, if I repent.

E. ANGEL. Ay, but Faustus never shall repent.
                              [*Exeunt* ANGELS.]

40   FAUST. My heart's so hardened I cannot repent.
Scarce can I name salvation, faith, or heaven,
But fearful echoes thunder in mine ears:
"Faustus, thou art damned!" Then swords and knives,
Poison, guns, halters, and envenomed steel
Are laid before me to dispatch myself,
And long ere this I should have slain myself
Had not sweet pleasure conquered deep despair.
Have I not made blind Homer sing to me
Of Alexander's love and Oenon's death,

50 And hath not he that built the walls of Thebes

44 **halters** hangman's ropes 45 **dispatch** kill 49 **Alexander**
Paris, son of Priam and lover of Oenone, whom he later
abandoned 50 **he** Amphion

With ravishing sound of his melodious harp
Made music with my Mephistophilis?
Why should I die, then, or basely despair?
I am resolved Faustus shall ne'er repent.
Come, Mephistophilis, let us dispute again
And argue of divine astrology.
Tell me, are there many heavens above the moon?
Are all celestial bodies but one globe
As is the substance of this centric earth?

MEPH. As are the elements, such are the spheres, 60
Mutually folded in each other's orb;
And jointly move upon one axletree
Whose terminine is termed the world's wide pole;
Nor are the names of Saturn, Mars, or Jupiter
Feigned, but are erring stars.

FAUST. But tell me, have they all one motion, both
situ et tempore?

MEPH. All jointly move from East to West in 24
hours upon the poles of the world, but differ in their
motion upon the poles of the zodiac.   70

FAUST. Tush,
These slender trifles Wagner can decide.
Hath Mephistophilis no greater skill?
Who knows not the double motion of the planets?
The first is finished in a natural day;

56 **astrology** astronomy 57 **heavens** rotating spheres 58 **Are
all . . . Is** the entire universe a ball? 59 **centric** central 60
elements fire, air, water, earth, arranged in concentric circles
with earth at the center 62 **axletree** axis 63 **terminine** terminus
65 **erring** wandering; pun on the amorous escapades of the
gods whose names the planets bore 67 **situ et tempore** in
direction and in period of revolution 70 **zodiac** circular belt
of the sky within which the sun ran its annual path around the
earth in the Ptolemaic astronomy 74 **double motion** the east-
west daily complete rotation of all planets around the earth,
and the much slower west-east rotation of each in its own
sphere

The second thus, as Saturn in 30 years, Jupiter in 12, Mars in 4, the Sun, Venus, and Mercury in a year, the Moon in 28 days. Tush, these are freshmen's suppositions. But tell me, hath every sphere a do-
80 minion or *Intelligentia?*

MEPH. Ay.

FAUST. How many heavens or spheres are there?

MEPH. Nine: the seven planets, the firmament, and the empyreal heaven.

FAUST. But is there not *coelum igneum, et crystallinum?*

MEPH. No, Faustus, they be but fables.

FAUST. Well, resolve me in this question: why have we not conjunctions, oppositions, aspects,
90 eclipses, all at one time, but in some years we have more, in some less?

MEPH. *Per inequalem motum respectu totius.*

FAUST. Well, I am answered. Tell me, who made the world?

MEPH. I will not.

FAUST. Sweet Mephistophilis, tell me.

MEPH. Move me not, for I will not tell thee.

FAUST. Villain, have I not bound thee to tell me anything?

100   MEPH. Ay, that is not against our kingdom; but this is.

Think thou on hell, Faustus, for thou art damned.

FAUST. Think, Faustus, upon God that made the world!

80 **dominion or Intelligentia** governing spirit or angelic intelligence 83 **firmament** heaven of fixed stars 84 **empyreal** God's habitation 85 **coelum . . . crystallinum** a sphere of fire and a crystalline sphere 89 **conjunctions, etc.** friendly or hostile positions of planets according to astrology 92 **per inequalem . . .** because of their dissimilar rates of motion with regard to the whole universe 97 **move** ask

MEPH. Remember this!   *Exit.*

FAUST. Ay, go, accursèd spirit, to ugly hell;
'Tis thou has damned distressèd Faustus' soul.
Is't not too late?

Enter GOOD ANGEL *and* EVIL ANGEL.

E. ANGEL. Too late.

G. ANGEL. Never too late, if Faustus can repent.

E. ANGEL. If thou repent, devils shall tear thee in 110
pieces.

G. ANGEL. Repent, and they shall never raze thy
skin.   *Exeunt* ANGELS.

FAUST. Ah Christ, my Savior!
Seek to save distressèd Faustus' soul.

Enter LUCIFER, BELZEBUB, *and* MEPHISTOPHILIS.

LUC. Christ cannot save thy soul, for he is just;
There's none but I have interest in the same.

FAUST. O who art thou that lookst so terrible?

LUC. I am Lucifer,
And this is my companion prince in hell.   120

FAUST. O Faustus, they are come to fetch away thy
soul!

LUC. We come to tell thee thou dost injure us:
Thou call'st on Christ, contrary to thy promise.
Thou shouldst not think of God; think of the devil,—
And of his dam too.

FAUST. Nor will I henceforth. Pardon me in this,
And Faustus vows never to look to heaven,
Never to name God or to pray to him,
To burn his Scripture, slay his ministers,   130
And make my spirits pull his churches down.

LUC. Do so, and we will highly gratify thee.

112 **raze** scratch 117 **interest** legal title 123 **injure** wrong
126 **dam** mother 132 **gratify** reward

Faustus, we are come from hell to show thee some pastime: sit down, and thou shalt see all the Seven Deadly Sins appear in their proper shapes.

FAUST. That sight will be as pleasing unto me as paradise was to Adam, the first day of his creation.

LUC. Talk not of paradise nor creation, but mark
140   this show; talk of the devil and nothing else. Come, away!

Enter the SEVEN DEADLY SINS.

Now, Faustus, examine them of their several names and dispositions.

FAUST. That shall I soon. What art thou, the first?

PRIDE. I am Pride. I disdain to have any parents. I am like to Ovid's flea: I can creep into every corner of a wench; sometimes like a periwig I sit upon her brow; next like a necklace I hang about her neck, or like a fan of feathers I kiss her lips; and then turning
150 myself to a wrought smock do what I list. But fie, what a scent is here! I'll not speak another word except the ground were perfumed and covered with cloth of arras.

FAUST. Thou art a proud knave indeed. What art thou, the second?

COVET. I am Covetousness, begotten of an old churl in an old leathern bag; and, might I have my wish, I would desire that this house and all the people in it were turned to gold, that I might lock you up in my
160 chest. O my sweet gold!

FAUST. What art thou, the third?

WRATH. I am Wrath. I had neither father nor mother; I leaped out of a lion's mouth when I was

147 **periwig** wig, false hair   150 **wrought smock** embroidered dress **list** wish   153 **arras** tapestry   156 **of** by **churl** miser   157 **leathern bag** leather suit, also leather purse

scarce half an hour old, and ever since I have run up
and down the world with this case of rapiers, wound-
ing myself when I had nobody to fight withal. I was
born in hell; and look to it, for some of you shall be
my father.

FAUST. What art thou, the fourth?

ENVY. I am Envy, begotten of a chimney-sweeper 170
and an oyster-wife. I cannot read, and therefore wish
all books were burned. I am lean with seeing others
eat. O that there would come a famine through all
the world, that all might die, and I live alone; then
thou shouldst see how fat I would be! But must thou
sit and I stand? Come down, with a vengeance!

FAUST. Away, envious rascal! What art thou, the
fifth?

GLUT. Who, I, sir? I am Gluttony. My parents are
all dead, and the devil a penny they have left me but 180
a bare pension, and that is 30 meals a day and ten
bevers—a small trifle to suffice nature. O I come of a
royal parentage: my grandfather was a gammon of
bacon, my grandmother a hogshead of claret wine.
My godfathers were these: Peter Pickle-herring and
Martin Martlemas-beef. O but my godmother—she
was a jolly gentlewoman, and well beloved in every
good town and city: her name was mistress Margery
March-beer. Now, Faustus, thou hast heard all my
progeny; wilt thou bid me to supper? 190

FAUST. No, I'll see thee hanged! Thou wilt eat up
all my victuals.

GLUT. Then the devil choke thee.

165 **case** couple 171 **oyster-wife** woman oyster vender 176
vengeance curse on you 182 **bevers** snacks 183 **gammon**
bottom piece of a flitch of bacon 186 **Martlemas-beef** salt beef
hung up on St. Martin's day 189 **March-beer** ale made in
March 190 **progeny** ancestry

FAUST. Choke thyself, glutton. What art thou, the sixth?

SLOTH. I am Sloth. I was begotten on a sunny bank, where I have lain ever since, and you have done me great injury to bring me from thence; let me be car-ried thither again by Gluttony and Lechery. I'll not
200 speak another word for a king's ransom.

FAUST. What are you, mistress minx, the seventh and last?

LECHERY. Who, I, sir? I am one that loves an inch of raw mutton better than an ell of fried stockfish, and the first letter of my name begins with L—echery.

LUC. Away, to hell, to hell!   *Exeunt the* SINS.
Now, Faustus, how dost thou like this?

FAUST. O this feeds my soul!

LUC. Tut, Faustus, in hell is all manner of delight.
210 FAUST. O that I might see hell and return again, how happy were I then!

LUC. Thou shalt. I will send for thee at midnight. In mean time take this book, peruse it thoroughly, and thou shalt turn thyself into what shape thou wilt.

FAUST. Great thanks, mighty Lucifer;
This will I keep as chary as my life.

LUC. Farewell, Faustus, and think on the devil.

FAUST. Farewell, great Lucifer. Come, Mephi-
220 stophilis.   *Exeunt omnes.*

204 **mutton** a loose woman **ell** 45 inches **stockfish** dried cod
217 **chary** carefully

Scene VII

❧

Enter WAGNER *solus, as Chorus.*

WAG. Learned Faustus,
To know the secrets of astronomy
Graven in the book of Jove's high firmament,
Did mount himself to scale Olympus' top.
Being seated in a chariot burning bright
Drawn by the strength of yokéd dragons' necks,
He views the clouds, the planets, and the stars,
The tropic zones and quarters of the sky
From the bright circle of the horned moon
Even to the height of *Primum Mobile;*   10
And whirling round with this circumference
Within the concave compass of the pole,
From east to west his dragons swiftly glide
And in eight days did bring him home again.
Not long he stayed within his quiet house
To rest his bones after his weary toil
But new exploits do hale him out again;
And mounted then upon a dragon's back
That with his wings did part the subtle air,
He now is gone to prove cosmography   20
That measures coasts and kingdoms of the earth:
And, as I guess, will first arrive at Rome
To see the Pope and manner of his court

8 **tropic zones** regions between the tropics of Capricorn and
Cancer 10 **Primum Mobile** outermost moving heaven 12 **concave compass** concave outer limits revolving about the axis of
the universe 17 **hale** bring 20 **prove** verify **cosmography** the
science that maps the cosmos as a whole

And take some part of holy Peter's feast,
The which this day is highly solemnized.

Exit WAGNER.

Enter FAUSTUS *and* MEPHISTOPHILIS.

FAUST. Having now, my good Mephistophilis,
Passed with delight the stately town of Trier
Environed round with airy mountain tops,
With walls of flint and deep-entrenched lakes,
30 Not to be won by any conquering prince;
From Paris next coasting the realm of France,
We saw the river Maine fall into Rhine,
Whose banks are set with groves of fruitful vines;
Then up to Naples, rich Campania,
Whose buildings fair and gorgeous to the eye,
The streets straight forth and paved with finest brick
Quarters the town in four equivalents.
There saw we learned Maro's golden tomb,
The way he cut, an English mile in length,
40 Thorough a rock of stone in one night's space.
From thence to Venice, Padua, and the rest,
In midst of which a sumptuous temple stands
That threats the stars with her aspiring top,
Whose frame is paved with sundry colored stones
And roofed aloft with curious work in gold.
Thus hitherto hath Faustus spent his time.
But tell me now, what resting place is this?
Hast thou, as erst I did command,
Conducted me within the walls of Rome?
50　MEPH. Faustus, I have; and because we will not be
　　　unprovided,

24 **Peter's feast** St. Peter's day, June 29　25 **solemnized** cele-
brated　27 **Trier** Treves on the Mosel River　29 **lakes** moats　34
Campania Campagna, a province in Italy　36 **straight forth** in
straight lines　37 **equivalents** equal parts　38 **Maro** Vergil,
Roman poet, believed in medieval times to have been a magician　42 **temple** perhaps St. Mark's in Venice　48 **erst** formerly

I have taken up his Holiness' privy chamber for our
    use.

  FAUST. I hope his Holiness will bid us welcome.

  MEPH. Tut, 'tis no matter, man; we'll be bold with
    his good cheer.

And now, my Faustus, that thou may'st perceive
What Rome containeth to delight thee with,
Know that this city stands upon seven hills
That underprops the groundwork of the same;
Just through the midst runs flowing Tiber's
    stream,
With winding banks that cut it in two parts,
Over the which four stately bridges lean   60
That makes safe passage to each part of Rome.
Upon the bridge called Ponto Angelo
Erected is a castle passing strong,
Within whose walls such store of ordnance are,
And double cannons framed of carved brass,
As match the days within one complete year—
Besides the gates and high pyramides
Which Julius Caesar brought from Africa.

  FAUST. Now by the kingdoms of infernal rule,
Of Styx, Acheron, and the fiery lake   70
Of ever-burning Phlegethon, I swear
That I do long to see the monuments
And situation of bright-splendent Rome.
Come, therefore, let's away.

  MEPH. Nay, Faustus, stay; I know you'd fain see
    the Pope
And take some part of holy Peter's feast,
Where thou shalt see a troop of bald-pate friars
Whose *summum bonum* is in belly-cheer.

51 **privy** private 64 **store** abundance **ordnance** war materials
65 **double cannons** cannons with double bores 67 **pyramides**
obelisk 73 **bright-splendent** brightly shining 78 **summum
bonum** highest ideal

FAUST. Well, I am content to compass then some
        sport
80 And by their folly make us merriment.
   Then charm me that I may be invisible,
   To do what I please
   Unseen of any whilst I stay in Rome.

                        [MEPHISTOPHILIS *charms him.*]

   MEPH. So, Faustus; now
   Do what thou wilt thou shalt not be discerned.

Sound a sennet. Enter the POPE *and the* CARDINAL
OF LORRAINE *to the banquet, with* FRIARS *attending.*

   POPE. My Lord of Lorraine, will't please you draw
   near?

   FAUST. Fall to, and the devil choke you and you
   spare.

90   POPE. How now, who's that which spake? Friars
   look about.

   FRIAR. Here's nobody, if it like your Holiness.

   POPE. My lord, here is a dainty dish was sent me
   from the Bishop of Milan.

   FAUST. I thank you, sir.   *Snatch it.*

   POPE. How now, who's that which snatched the
   meat from me? Will no man look? My lord, this dish
   was sent me from the Cardinal of Florence.

100   FAUST. You say true; I'll ha't.   [*Snatch it.*]

   POPE. What, again! My lord, I'll drink to your
   grace.

   FAUST. I'll pledge your grace.   [*Snatch it.*]

   LORR. My Lord, it may be some ghost newly crept
   out of Purgatory come to beg a pardon of your Holiness.

79 **compass** bring about 85 **sennet** fanfare of trumpets 88 **Fall
to** begin eating **and** if 92 **like** please 103 **pledge** drink to 105
beg a pardon ask the Pope for an official pardon for sin, short-
ening the ghost's punishments in Purgatory

POPE. It may be so. Friars, prepare a dirge to lay
the fury of this ghost. Once again, my lord, fall to.

The POPE *crosseth himself.*

FAUST. What, are you crossing of your self?
Well, use that trick no more, I would advise you.   110

Cross again.

Well, that's the second time. Aware the third,
I give you fair warning.

Cross again, and FAUSTUS *hits him a
box of the ear, and they all run away.*

FAUST. Come on, Mephistophilis, what shall we
do?

MEPH. Nay, I know not; we shall be cursed with
bell, book and candle.

FAUST. How! bell, book, and candle, candle, book,
and bell,

Forward and backward to curse Faustus to hell.

Anon you shall hear a hog grunt, a calf bleat, and an
ass bray,

Because it is Saint Peter's holy day.   120

Enter all the FRIARS *to sing the dirge.*

FRIAR. Come, brethren, let's about our business
with good devotion.

All sing this:

Cursed be he that stole away his Holiness' meat
from the table—*maledicat dominus!*

Cursed be he that struck his Holiness a blow on
the face—*maledicat dominus!*

Cursed be he that took Friar Sandelo a blow on
the face—*maledicat dominus!*

Cursed be he that disturbeth our holy dirge—
maledicat dominus!

107 **lay** calm 116 **bell, book and candle** used by the Roman
Catholic church in the ceremony of excommunication 123
maledicat dominus may God curse him

130   Cursed be he that took away his Holiness' wine—
        maledicat dominus! Et omnes sancti! Amen.
                    Beat the FRIARS, *and fling fire-*
                works among them, and so exeunt.

Scene VIII

❦

Enter ROBIN *the Ostler with a book in his hand.*

ROB. O this is admirable! Here I ha' stolen one of
Doctor Faustus' conjuring books, and, i'faith, I mean
to search some circles for my own use: now will I
make all the maidens in our parish dance at my pleasure stark naked before me, and so by that means I
shall see more that e'er I felt or saw yet.

Enter RALPH *calling* ROBIN.

RALPH. Robin, prithee come away; there's a gentleman tarries to have his horse, and he would have his
things rubbed and made clean. He keeps such a
10 chafing with my mistress about it, and she has sent
me to look thee out; prithee, come away.

ROB. Keep out, keep out, or else you are blown up,
you are dismembered, Ralph; keep out, for I am
about a roaring piece of work.

RALPH. Come, what doest thou with that same

131 **et omnes sancti** and all the saints   3 **search some circles**
find some formulae for drawing a conjuror's circles; also a
pornographic pun, as in many of the other words in this scene
10 **chafing** quarreling   11 **look thee out** find you

book? Thou canst not read.

ROB. Yes, my master and mistress shall find that I can read—he for his forehead, she for her private study. She's born to bear with me, or else my art fails.

RALPH. Why, Robin, what book is that?   20

ROB. What book? Why the most intolerable book for conjuring that e'er was invented by any brimstone devil.

RALPH. Canst thou conjure with it?

ROB. I can do all these things easily with it: first, I can make thee drunk with ippocras at any tavern in Europe for nothing; that's one of my conjuring works.

RALPH. Our master Parson says that's nothing.

ROB. True, Ralph; and more, Ralph, if thou hast 30 any mind to Nan Spit our kitchen maid, then turn her and wind her to thy own use as often as thou wilt, and at midnight.

RALPH. O brave, Robin! Shall I have Nan Spit, and to mine own use? On that condition I'll feed thy devil with horse-bread as long as he lives, of free cost.

ROB. No more, sweet Ralph. Let's go and make clean our boots which lie foul upon our hands, and then to our conjuring in the devil's name.   *Exeunt.* 40

18 **forehead** where the horns of the cuckold grew 26 **ippocras** spiced wine with sugar 35 **horse-bread** coarse bread fed to horses

Scene IX

✶

Enter ROBIN *and* RALPH *with a silver goblet.*

ROB. Come, Ralph, did I not tell thee we were forever made by this Doctor Faustus' book? *Ecce signum:* here's a simple purchase for horse-keepers! Our horses shall eat no hay as long as this lasts.

Enter the VINTNER.

RALPH. But Robin, here comes the vintner.

ROB. Hush, I'll gull him supernaturally. Drawer, I hope all is paid; God be with you. Come, Ralph.

VINT. Soft, sir, a word with you: I must yet have a goblet paid from you ere you go.

10   ROB. I a goblet? Ralph—I a goblet? I scorn you, and you are but a etc. I a goblet? Search me.

VINT. I mean so, sir, with your favor.

[*Searches* ROBIN.]

ROB. How say you now?

VINT. I must say somewhat to your fellow: you sir.   [*Searches* RALPH.]

RALPH. Me, sir? Search your fill. Now, sir, you may be ashamed to burden honest men with a matter of truth.

VINT. Well, t'one of you hath this goblet about you.

20   ROB. [*Aside.*] You lie, drawer, 'tis afore me.—Sirrah

2 **Ecce signum** behold proof 3 **simple purchase** small acquisition ‚5 **vintner** innkeeper selling wine 6 **gull** fool **supernaturally** extraordinarily **drawer** one who serves liquor to customers 7 **all** the whole bill 11 **etc.** the clown adlibs here 12 **favor** leave 17 **burden** accuse them of lying 20 **afore** in front of

you, I'll teach ye to impeach honest men! Stand by:
I'll scour you for a goblet; stand aside, you had best,
I charge you in the name of Belzebub. [*Aside.*] Look
to the goblet, Ralph.

VINT. What mean you, sirrah?

ROB. I'll tell you what I mean: *Reads*
Sanctobulorum Periphrasticon—nay, I'll tickle you,
          vintner. [*Aside*] Look to the goblet, Ralph.
Polypragmos Belseborams framanto pacostiphos
          tostu Mephistophilis etc.

Enter MEPHISTOPHILIS, *sets squibs at their backs* [*and*
          withdraws]. *They run about.*

VINT. *O nomine Domine!* what meanest thou,
Robin? Thou hast no goblet.   30

RALPH. *Peccatum peccatorum!* here's thy goblet,
good vintner.

ROB. *Misericordia pro nobis!* what shall I do? Good
devil, forgive me now and I'll never rob thy library
more.

          Re-enter to them MEPHISTOPHILIS.

MEPH. Vanish, villains! th' one like an ape, another
          like a bear, the third an ass, for doing this enter-
          prise.   [*Exit* VINTNER.]
Monarch of hell, under whose black survey
Great potentates do kneel with awful fear,
Upon whose altars thousand souls do lie,
How am I vexéd with these villains' charms!   **40**
From Constantinople am I hither come

22 **scour** clean, also purge 27 **Sanctobulorum . . .** nonsense
consisting of corrupt Latin and Greek words s d **squibs fire-**
crackers 29 **nomine Domine** in God's name (corrupt) 31
peccatum peccatorum sinners that we are (corrupt) 33 **Miseri-**
cordia . . . have pity on us 36 **like** in the shape of 37 **survey**
gaze 38 **awful** full of awe

Only for pleasure of these damned slaves.

Rob. How, from Constantinople? You have had a great journey: will you take sixpence in your purse to pay for your supper, and be gone?

Meph. Well, villains, for your presumption I transform thee into an ape, and thee into a dog; and so be gone.   *Exit.*

Rob. How, into an ape? That's brave: I'll have fine
50 sport with the boys; I'll get nuts and apples enow.

Ralph. And I must be a dog.

Rob. I'faith, thy head will never be out of the pottage-pot.   *Exeunt.*

Scene X

❧

Enter Chorus.

Chorus. When Faustus had with pleasure ta'en the
  view
Of rarest things and royal courts of kings,
He stayed his course and so returnéd home,
Where such as bear his absence but with grief,
I mean his friends and nearest companiöns,
Did gratulate his safety with kind words,
And in their conference of what befell
Touching his journey through the world and air,
They put forth questions of astrology
10 Which Faustus answered with such learned skill

49 **brave** fine 50 **enow** enough 52 **pottage** thick soup 4 **but**
only 6 **gratulate** congratulate 7 **conference** talk 9 **astrology**
astronomy

As they admired and wondered at his wit.
Now is his fame spread forth in every land:
Amongst the rest the Emperor is one,
Carolus the Fifth, at whose palace now
Faustus is feasted mongst his noblemen.
What there he did in trial of his art
I leave untold, your eyes shall see performed.

Enter EMPEROR, FAUSTUS, MEPHISTOPHILIS, *and a*
KNIGHT, *with* ATTENDANTS.

EMP. Master Doctor Faustus, I have heard strange
report of thy knowledge in the black art, how that
none in my empire nor in the whole world can com- 20
pare with thee for the rare effects of magic. They say
thou hast a familiar spirit, by whom thou canst ac-
complish what thou list. This, therefore, is my request, that thou let me see some proof of thy skill,
that mine eyes may be witnesses to confirm what
mine ears have heard reported; and here I swear to
thee, by the honor of mine imperial crown, that whatever thou doest thou shalt be no ways prejudiced or
endamaged.

KNIGHT. [*Aside.*] I'faith, he looks much like a con- 30
juror.

FAUST. My gracious Sovereign, though I must confess myself far inferior to the report men have published, and nothing answerable to the honor of your
imperial Majesty, yet for that love and duty binds
me thereunto, I am content to do whatsover your
majesty shall command me.

EMP. Then, Doctor Faustus, mark what I shall say:
As I was sometime solitary set
Within my closet, sundry thoughts arose   40
About the honor of mine ancestors—

14 **Carolus** Charles V, Emperor of Germany 34 **nothing answerable** quite unequal to 39 **set** seated 40 **closet** private
chamber

How they had won by prowess such exploits,
Got such riches, subdued so many kingdoms,
As we that do succeed or they that shall
Hereafter possess our throne shall,
I fear me, never attain to that degree
Of high renown and great authority.
Amongst which kings is Alexander the great,
Chief spectacle of the world's pre-eminence,

50 The bright shining of whose glorious acts
Lightens the world with his reflecting beams,
As when I hear but motion made of him
It grieves my soul I never saw the man.
If, therefore, thou by cunning of thine art
Canst raise this man from hollow vaults below
Where lies entombed this famous conqueror,
And bring him with his beauteous paramour,
Both in their right shapes, gesture, and attire
They used to wear during their time of life,

60 Thou shalt both satisfy my just desire
And give me cause to praise thee whilst I live.

    FAUST. My gracious Lord, I am ready to accomplish your request, so far forth as by art and power of my spirit I am able to perform.

    KNIGHT. [*Aside.*] I'faith, that's just nothing at all.

    FAUST. But if it like your Grace, it is not in my ability to present before your eyes the true substantial bodies of those two deceased princes which long since are consumed to dust.

70   KNIGHT. [*Aside.*] Ay marry, Master Doctor, now there's a sign of grace in you, when you will confess the truth.

    FAUST. But such spirits as can lively resemble Alex-

44 succeed inherit the throne   **49 world's pre-eminence** men pre-eminent in the world   **52 motion** mention   **54 cunning** skill   **57 paramour** mistress   **67 true substantial** true substance of the bodies   **73 lively** in a lifelike way

ander and his paramour shall appear before your Grace, in that manner that they best lived in in their most flourishing estate, which I doubt not shall sufficiently content your imperial Majesty.

EMP. Go to, Master Doctor; let me see them presently.

KNIGHT. Do you hear, Master Doctor, you bring 80 Alexander and his paramour before the Emperor?

FAUST. How then, sir?

KNIGHT. I'faith, that's true as Diana turned me to a stag.

FAUST. No, sir, but when Actaeon died he left the horns for you. Mephistophilis, be gone!

Exit MEPHISTOPHILIS.

KNIGHT. Nay, and you go to conjuring I'll be gone.

Exit KNIGHT.

FAUST. I'll meet with you anon for interrupting me so.—

Here they are, my gracious Lord.

Enter MEPHISTOPHILIS *with* [*spirits as*] ALEXANDER
and his paramour.

EMP. Master Doctor, I heard this lady while she 90 lived had a wart or mole in her neck. How shall I know whether it be so or no?

FAUST. Your Highness may boldly go and see.

[EMPEROR *sees the mole; then spirits exeunt.*]

EMP. Sure these are no spirits but the true substantial bodies of those two deceased princes.

FAUST. Will't please your Highness now to send for the knight that was so pleasant with me here of late?

EMP. One of you call him forth.

78 **presently** without delay 85 **Actaeon** lover of Diana turned by her into a stag 87 **and** if 88 **meet** get even

Enter the KNIGHT *with a pair of horns on his head.*

100 EMP. How now, sir knight! Why, I had thought thou hadst been a bachelor, but now I see thou hast a wife that not only gives thee horns but makes thee wear them. Feel on thy head.

KNIGHT. Thou damned wretch and execrable dog
Bred in the concave of some monstrous rock,
How dar'st thou thus abuse a gentleman?
Villain, I say, undo what thou hast done!

FAUST. O not so fast, sir; there's no haste but good. Are you remembered how you crossed me in my con-
110 ference with the Emperor? I think I have met with you for it.

EMP. Good Master Doctor, at my entreaty release him; he hath done penance sufficient.

FAUST. My gracious Lord, not so much for the injury he offered me here in your presence, as to delight you with some mirth hath Faustus worthily requited this injurious knight, which being all I desire, I am content to release him of his horns. And, sir knight, hereafter speak well of scholars. Mephistoph-
120 ilis, transform him straight. Now, good my Lord, having done my duty I humbly take my leave.

EMP. Farewell, Master Doctor; yet ere you go expect from me a bounteous reward.   [*Exeunt.*]

101 **bachelor** novice knight, also unmarried man 108 **no haste but good** proverb meaning 'what's your hurry?'

Scene XI

Enter FAUSTUS *and* MEPHISTOPHILIS.

FAUST. Now, Mephistophilis, the restless course
That time doth run with calm and silent foot,
Short'ning my days and thread of vital life,
Calls for the payment of my latest years.
Therefore, sweet Mephistophilis, let us
Make haste to Wittenberg.
  MEPH. What, will you go on horseback or on foot?
  FAUST. Nay, till I am past this fair and pleasant
    green
I'll walk on foot.

Enter a HORSE-COURSER.

HORSE-C. I have been all this day seeking one Mas- 10
ter Fustian: mass, see where he is!—God save you,
Master Doctor.
  FAUST. What, horse-courser, you are well met.
  HORSE-C. Do you hear, sir, I have brought you
forty dollars for your horse.
  FAUST. I cannot sell him so; if thou lik'st him for
fifty, take him.
  HORSE-C. Alas, sir, I have no more. [*To* MEPHI-
STOPHILIS.] I pray you speak for me.
  MEPH. I pray you, let him have him: he is an hon- 20
est fellow, and he has a great charge [*Aside.*] neither
wife nor child.
  FAUST. Well, come, give me your money. My boy
will deliver him to you; but I must tell you one thing
21 **charge** family responsibility

before you have him: ride him not into the water at any hand.

HORSE-C. Why, sir, will he not drink of all waters?

FAUST. O yes, he will drink of all waters, but ride him not into the water. Ride him over hedge or
30 ditch, or where thou wilt, but not into the water.

HORSE-C. Well, sir, now am I made man forever: I'll not leave my horse for forty. If he had but the quality of hey ding, hey ding ding, I'd make a brave living on him: he has a buttock as slick as an eel. Well, God b'wi'ye, sir, your boy will deliver him me—but hark ye, sir, if my horse be sick or ill at ease, if I bring his water to you you'll tell me what it is?

FAUST. Away, you villain! What, dost think I am a
    horse-doctor?   *Exit* HORSE-COURSER.
What art thou, Faustus, but a man condemned to
    die?
40 Thy fatal time doth draw to final end,
Despair doth drive distrust unto my thoughts.
Confound these passions with a quiet sleep:
Tush, Christ did call the thief upon the cross;
Then rest thee, Faustus, quiet in conceit.

                Sleep in his chair.

Enter HORSE-COURSER *all wet, crying.*

HORSE-C. Alas, alas, Doctor Fustian quotha! Mass, Doctor Lopus was never such a doctor; he has given me a purgation, has purged me of forty dollars; I shall never see them more. But yet, like an ass as I was, I would not be ruled by him, for he bade me

25-26 **at any hand** under any circumstances 32 **leave** sell 33 **hey ding** refrain of popular love songs; here probably means the quality of being a good stud horse 37 **water** urine 42 **confound** conquer 43 **call** give salvation to 44 **conceit** mind 46 **Lopus** Lopez, prominent Jewish physician hanged for treason in 1594 47 **has** he has 49 **ruled** take his advice

I should ride him into no water. Now I, thinking my 50
horse had had some rare quality that he would not
have had me know of, I, like a venturous youth, rid
him into the deep pond at the town's end. I was no
sooner in the middle of the pond but my horse van-
ished away, and I sat upon a bottle of hay, never so
near drowning in my life. But I'll seek out my Doctor
and have my forty dollars again, or I'll make it the
dearest horse!—O, yonder is his snipper-snapper.
[*To* MEPHISTOPHILIS.] Do you hear, you hey-pass,
where's your master? 60

MEPH. Why, sir, what would you? You cannot
speak with him.

HORSE-C. But I will speak with him.

MEPH. Why, he's fast asleep; come some other
time.

HORSE-C. I'll speak with him now, or I'll break his
glass-windows about his ears.

MEPH. I tell thee, he has not slept this eight nights.

HORSE-C. And he have not slept this eight weeks
I'll speak with him. 70

MEPH. See where he is, fast asleep.

HORSE-C. Ay, this is he. God save ye, Master Doctor. Master Doctor! Master Doctor Fustian! Forty
dollars, forty dollars for a bottle of hay!

MEPH. Why, thou seest he hears thee not.

HORSE-C. So ho ho! So ho ho!   *Hallow in his ear.*
No, will you not wake? I'll make you wake ere I go.
          Pull him by the leg, and pull it away.
Alas, I am undone! What shall I do?

FAUST. O my leg, my leg! Help, Mephistophilis:
call the officers! My leg, my leg! 80

MEPH. Come, villain, to the Constable.

55 **bottle** bundle 58 **dearest** most expensive **snipper-snapper**
serving-man 59 **hey-pass** juggler 67 **glass-windows** spectacles

Horse-C. O Lord, sir, let me go, and I'll give you forty dollars more.

Meph. Where be they?

Horse-C. I have none about me; come to my ostry and I'll give them to you.

Meph. Be gone quickly.

Horse-Courser runs away.

Faust. What, is he gone? Farewell he! Faustus has his leg again, and the Horse-courser, I take it, a bot-
90 tle of hay for his labor. Well, this trick shall cost him forty dollars more.

Enter Wagner.

How now, Wagner, what's the news with thee?

Wag. Sir, the Duke of Vanholt doth earnestly entreat your company.

Faust. The Duke of Vanholt!—an honorable gentleman, to whom I must be no niggard of my cunning. Come, Mephistophilis, let's away to him.

Exeunt.

Scene XII

❧

Re-enter Faustus and Mephistophilis with the
Duke <i>and</i> Duchess of Vanholt.</div>

Duke. Believe me, Master Doctor, this merriment hath much pleased me.

Faust. My gracious Lord, I am glad it contents you so well. But it may be, Madam, you take no delight

85 ostry inn

in this. I have heard that great-bellied women do
long for some dainties or other: what is it, Madam?
Tell me, and you shall have it.

DUCH. Thanks, good Master Doctor; and for I see
your courteous intent to pleasure me, I will not hide
from you the thing my heart desires, and were it now 10
summer, as it is January and the dead time of the
winter, I would desire no better meat than a dish of
ripe grapes.

FAUST. Alas, Madam, that's nothing. Mephistoph-
    ilis, be gone!   [*Exit* MEPHISTOPHILIS.]
Were it a greater thing than this, so it would content
    you you should have it.

    Re-enter MEPHISTOPHILIS *with the grapes.*

Here they be, Madam: will't please you taste on
    them?

DUCH. Believe me, Master Doctor, this makes me
wonder above the rest, that being in the dead time
of winter and in the month of January, how you
should come by these grapes.   20

FAUST. If it like your Grace, the year is divided into
two circles over the whole world, that when it is here
winter with us in the contrary circle it is summer
with them, as in India, Saba, and farther countries
in the East, and, by means of a swift spirit that I
have, I had them brought hither as ye see. How do
you like them, Madam? be they good?

DUCH. Believe me, Master Doctor, they be the best
grapes that e'er I tasted in my life before.

FAUST. I am glad they content you so, Madam.   30
    DUKE. Come, Madam, let us in,
Where you must well reward this learned man
For the great kindness he hath showed to you.

5 **great-bellied** pregnant 12 **meat** food 16 **on** of 23 **circle**
hemisphere 24 **Saba** Sheba

DUCH. And so I will, my Lord, and whilst I live
Rest beholding for this courtesy.

FAUST. I humbly thank your Grace.

DUCH. Come, Master Doctor, follow us and receive
your reward.   *Exeunt.*

Scene XIII

❧

Enter WAGNER *solus.*

WAG. I think my master means to die shortly
For he hath given to me all his goods;
And yet methinks if that death were near
He would not banquet, and carouse, and swill
Amongst the students, as even now he doth,
Who are at supper with such belly-cheer
As Wagner ne'er beheld in all his life.
See where they come: belike the feast is ended.
                                    [*Exit.*]

Enter FAUSTUS *and* MEPHISTOPHILIS *with two or three*
SCHOLARS.

1 SCH. Master Doctor Faustus, since our confer-
10 ence about fair ladies, which was the beautifullest in
all the world, we have determined with ourselves
that Helen of Greece was the admirablest lady that
ever lived. Therefore, Master Doctor, if you will do
us that favor as to let us see that peerless dame of
Greece whom all the world admires for majesty, we
should think ourselves much beholding unto you.

FAUST. Gentlemen,

33 **beholding** obliged

For that I know your friendship is unfeigned,
And Faustus' custom is not to deny
The just requests of those that wish him well,   20
You shall behold that peerless dame of Greece,
No otherways for pomp and majesty
Than when Sir Paris crossed the seas with her
And brought the spoils to rich Dardania.
Be silent, then, for danger is in words.

> *Music sounds, and* HELEN
> *passeth over the stage.*

2 SCH. Too simple is my wit to tell her praise
Whom all the world admires for majesty.

  3 SCH. No marvel though the angry Greeks pur-
    sued
With ten years' war the rape of such a queen
Whose heavenly beauty passeth all compare.   30

  1 SCH. Since we have seen the pride of Nature's
    works
And only paragon of excellence,
Let us depart, and for this glorious deed
Happy and blessed be Faustus evermore.

  FAUST. Gentlemen, farewell; the same I wish to
  you.   [*Exeunt* SCHOLARS.]

Enter an OLD MAN.

  OLD MAN. Ah, Doctor Faustus, that I might pre-
    vail
To guide thy steps unto the way of life,
By which sweet path thou may'st attain the goal
That shall conduct thee to celestial rest!
Break heart, drop blood, and mingle it with tears—   40
Tears falling from repentant heaviness
Of thy most vile and loathsome filthiness,
The stench whereof corrupts the inward soul

24 **Dardania** Troy 29 **rape** abduction 31 **pride** best

With such flagitious crimes of heinous sins
As no commiseration may expel
But mercy, Faustus, of thy Savior sweet,
Whose blood alone must wash away thy guilt.

    FAUST. Where art thou, Faustus? Wretch, what
      hast thou done?
Damned art thou, Faustus, damned! Despair and die.
50 Hell calls for right, and with a roaring voice
Says, "Faustus, come; thine hour is come!"
And Faustus will come to do thee right.

                    MEPHISTOPHILIS *gives him a dagger.*
    OLD MAN. Ah stay, good Faustus, stay thy des-
      perate steps!
I see an angel hovers o'er thy head
And with a vial full of precious grace
Offers to pour the same into thy soul:
Then call for mercy and avoid despair.

    FAUST. Ah my sweet friend, I feel thy words
To comfort my distressed soul.
60 Leave me awhile to ponder on my sins.

    OLD MAN. I go, sweet Faustus, but with heavy
      cheer,
Fearing the ruin of thy hopeless soul.   *[Exit.]*

    FAUST. Accurséd Faustus, where is mercy now?
I do repent and yet I do despair:
Hell strives with grace for conquest in my breast.
What shall I do to shun the snares of death?

    MEPH. Thou traitor, Faustus, I arrest thy soul
For disobedience to my sovereign lord.
Revolt, or I'll in piecemeal tear thy flesh.
70   FAUST. I do repent I e'er offended him.
Sweet Mephistophilis, entreat thy lord
To pardon my unjust presumption,
And with my blood again I will confirm

44 **flagitious** extremely wicked 50 **right** its rights 55 **grace**
God's grace 61 **cheer** mood 69 **revolt** deny God

My former vow I made to Lucifer.

MEPH. Do it then quickly with unfeigned heart
Lest greater danger do attend thy drift.

FAUST. Torment, sweet friend, that base and
    crooked age
That durst dissuade me from thy Lucifer,
With greatest torments that our hell affords.

MEPH. His faith is great: I cannot touch his soul;   80
But what I may afflict his body with
I will attempt, which is but little worth.

FAUST. One thing, good servant, let me crave of
    thee
To glut the longing of my heart's desire:
That I might have unto my paramour
That heavenly Helen which I saw of late,
Whose sweet embracings may extinguish clean
These thoughts that do dissuade me from my vow,
And keep mine oath I made to Lucifer.

MEPH. This, or what else my Faustus shall desire   90
Shall be performed in twinkling of an eye.

Enter HELEN.

FAUST. Was this the face that launched a thousand
    ships
And burnt the topless towers of Ilium?
Sweet Helen, make me immortal with a kiss.
Her lips sucks forth my soul—see where it flies!
Come, Helen, come, give me my soul again.
Here will I dwell, for heaven is in these lips
And all is dross that is not Helena.

Enter OLD MAN [*and stands watching* FAUSTUS.]

I will be Paris, and for love of thee
Instead of Troy shall Wittenberg be sacked,   100

76 drift delay **77 age** old man **93 Ilium** Troy

And I will combat with weak Menelaus
And wear thy colors on my pluméd crest;
Yea, I will wound Achilles in the heel
And then return to Helen for a kiss.
O thou art fairer than the evening air
Clad in the beauty of a thousand stars!
Brighter art thou than flaming Jupiter
When he appeared to hapless Semele,
More lovely than the monarch of the sky
110 In wanton Arethusa's azured arms,
And none but thou shalt be my paramour!

Exeunt all except the OLD MAN.

OLD MAN. Accursed Faustus, miserable man,
That from thy soul exclud'st the grace of heaven
And fliest the throne of his tribunal seat.

Enter the DEVILS *to torment him.*

Sathan begins to sift me with his pride.
As in this furnace God shall try my faith,
My faith, vile hell, shall triumph over thee!
Ambitious fiends, see how the heavens smiles
At your repulse, and laughs your state to scorn.
120 Hence, hell! for hence I fly unto my God.   *Exeunt.*

101 **Menelaus** husband of Helen 103 **Achilles** greatest of the
Greek champions against Troy 108 **Semele, Arethusa** women
embraced by the god Jupiter 115 **sift** test 119 **state** power

Scene XIV

❧

Enter FAUSTUS *with the* SCHOLARS.

FAUST. Ah, gentlemen!

1 SCH. What ails Faustus?

FAUST. Ah, my sweet chamber-fellow, had I lived with thee then had I lived still, but now I die eternally. Look! comes he not? comes he not?

2 SCH. What means Faustus?

3 SCH. Belike he is grown into some sickness by being over-solitary.

1 SCH. If it be so, we'll have physicians cure him; 'tis but a surfeit, never fear, man.   10

FAUST. A surfeit of deadly sin that hath damned both body and soul.

2 SCH. Yet, Faustus, look up to heaven: remember God's mercies are infinite.

FAUST. But Faustus' offence can ne'er be pardoned; the Serpent that tempted Eve may be saved, but not Faustus. Ah, gentlemen, hear me with patience, and tremble not at my speeches. Though my heart pants and quivers to remember that I have been a student here these thirty years, O would I had never seen 20 Wittenberg, never read book! And what wonders I have done all Germany can witness, yea all the world, for which Faustus hath lost both Germany and the world, yea heaven itself—heaven the seat of God, the throne of the blessed, the kingdom of joy, and must remain in hell forever, hell, ah hell, forever!

10 **surfeit** over-eating

Sweet friends, what shall become of Faustus, being in hell forever?

3 Sch. Yet, Faustus, call on God.

30 Faust. On God, whom Faustus hath abjured? on God, whom Faustus hath blasphemed? Ah, my God, I would weep, but the devil draws in my tears! Gush forth, blood, instead of tears, yea life and soul. O he stays my tongue; I would lift up my hands but, see, they hold them, they hold them!

All. Who, Faustus?

Faust. Lucifer and Mephistophilis.

Ah, gentlemen, I gave them my soul for my cunning.

All. God forbid!

40 Faust. God forbade it indeed, but Faustus hath done it: for vain pleasure of 24 years hath Faustus lost eternal joy and felicity. I writ them a bill with mine own blood, the date is expired, the time will come, and he will fetch me.

1 Sch. Why did not Faustus tell us of this before, that divines might have prayed for thee?

Faust. Oft have I thought to have done so, but the devil threatened to tear me in pieces if I named God, to fetch both body and soul if I once gave ear to 50 divinity; and now 'tis too late. Gentlemen, away, lest you perish with me.

2 Sch. O what shall we do to save Faustus?

Faust. Talk not of me, but save yourselves and depart.

3 Sch. God will strengthen me: I will stay with Faustus.

1 Sch. Tempt not God, sweet friend, but let us into the next room, and there pray for him.

Faust. Ay, pray for me, pray for me! And what 60 noise soever ye hear, come not unto me, for nothing can rescue me.

2 SCH. Pray thou, and we will pray that God may
have mercy upon thee.

FAUST. Gentlemen, farewell. If I live till morning
I'll visit you; if not, Faustus is gone to hell.

ALL. Faustus, farewell.   *Exeunt* SCHOLARS.
                                The clock strikes eleven.

FAUST. Ah, Faustus,
Now hast thou but one bare hour to live
And then thou must be damned perpetually!
Stand still, you ever-moving spheres of heaven,   70
That time may cease and midnight never come;
Fair Nature's eye, rise, rise again, and make
Perpetual day; or let this hour be but
A year, a month, a week, a natural day,
That Faustus may repent and save his soul!
O lente lente currite noctis equi.
The stars move still, time runs, the clock will strike,
The devil will come, and Faustus must be damned.
O I'll leap up to my God! Who pulls me down?
See, see, where Christ's blood streams in the firma-   80
     ment!—
One drop would save my soul—half a drop! ah, my
     Christ!
Ah, rend not my heart for naming of my Christ;
Yet will I call on him—Oh, spare me, Lucifer!
Where is it now? 'Tis gone; and see where God
Stretcheth out his arm and bends his ireful brows.
Mountains and hills, come, come and fall on me
And hide me from the heavy wrath of God,
That when you vomit forth into the air
My limbs may issue from your smoky mouths,
So that my soul may but ascend to heaven.   90
No, no—

72 **Nature's eye** the sun 74 **natural day** time from sunrise to
sunset 76 **lente** . . . slowly, run slowly, oh horses of the night

Then will I headlong run into the earth:
Earth, gape! O no, it will not harbor me.
You stars that reigned at my nativity,
Whose influence hath allotted death and hell,
Now draw up Faustus like a foggy mist
Into the entrails of yon laboring cloud
So that my soul may but ascend to heaven.

The watch strikes.

Ah, half the hour is past;
100 'Twill all be past anon.
O God,
If thou wilt not have mercy on my soul,
Yet for Christ's sake whose blood hath ransomed me
Impose some end to my incessant pain:
Let Faustus live in hell a thousand years,
A hundred thousand, and at last be saved!
O, no end is limited to damned souls.
Why wert thou not a creature wanting soul?
Or why is this immortal that thou hast?
110 Ah, Pythagoras' *metempsychosis*—were that true,
This soul should fly from me, and I be changed
Unto some brutish beast. All beasts are happy,
For when they die
Their souls are soon dissolved in elements,
But mine must live still to be plagued in hell.
Cursed be the parents that engendered me!
No, Faustus, curse thyself, curse Lucifer
That hath deprived thee of the joys of heaven.

The clock strikes twelve.

O it strikes, it strikes! Now, body, turn to air
120 Or Lucifer will bear thee quick to hell.

Thunder and lightning.

O soul, be changed into little water drops
And fall into the ocean, ne'er be found.

97 **laboring** heavy, stormy 110 **metempsychosis** transmigration
of souls from one body to another

My God, my God, look not so fierce on me!

[*Thunder.*] *Enter* Devils.

Adders and serpents, let me breathe awhile!
Ugly hell, gape not—come not, Lucifer—
I'll burn my books—ah, Mephistophilis!

Exeunt with him.

Enter Chorus.

Chorus. Cut is the branch that might have grown
        full straight,
And burnéd is Apollo's laurel bough
That sometime grew within this learned man.
Faustus is gone: regard his hellish fall,   130
Whose fiendful fortune may exhort the wise
Only to wonder at unlawful things
Whose deepness doth entice such forward wits
To practise more than heavenly power permits.

[*Exit.*]

Terminat hora diem, terminat author opus.

128 **Apollo** the god of learning 133 **forward wits** advanced in-
tellects **Terminat** . . . As the last hour ends the day, so the
author ends this work

BIBLIOGRAPHY

❦

EDITIONS

Boas, Frederick S., *The Tragical History of Doctor Faustus*, 1932.

Brooke, C. F. Tucker, *The Works of Christopher Marlowe*, 1910.

Rose, William, *The History of the Damnable Life and Deserved Death of Doctor John Faustus 1592*, 1925.

BIOGRAPHY AND CRITICISM

Boas, Frederick S., *Christopher Marlowe*, 1940.

Brooke, C. F. Tucker, *The Life of Marlowe*, 1930.

Eliot, T. S., *The Sacred Wood*, 1934.

Ellis-Fermor, U. M., *Christopher Marlowe*, 1927.

Hazlitt, William, Essay "On the Dramatic Writers Contemporary with Shakespear" in *Lectures on the Age of Elizabeth*.

Heilman, Robert B., "The Tragedy of Knowledge: Marlowe's Treatment of Faustus" in *Quarterly Review of Literature*, II (1946), 316-32.

Kirschbaum, Leo, "Marlowe's *Faustus:* A Reconsideration" in *Review of English Studies*, XIX (1943), 225-41.

Kocher, Paul H., *Christopher Marlowe*, 1946.

Simpson, Percy, "Marlowe's *Tragical History of Doctor Faustus*" in *Essays and Studies by Members of the English Association*, XIV (1929), 20-34.

Swinburne, Algernon C., Essay "Christopher Marlowe" in *The Age of Shakespeare*.